HOW TO DOMINATE RECRUITING IN A DIGITAL WORLD

A Guide for Recruiters, Leaders, and Recruiting Leaders

Richard Milligan

Paperback ISBN: 979-8-9866913-1-2
Hard Cover ISBN: 979-8-9866913-2-9

DEDICATION

This book is dedicated to the leaders who lived out their values in a way that attracted me to them. Many leaders simply pursue money and success. But you inspired me by revealing there was a more fulfilling way. Today I am a better leader and, thus, a better recruiting leader because of you. You are a ripple effect that keeps on impacting others. Pieces of this book are actually pieces of your life, your story, and the seasons we spent together. May I re-pay that investment forward in meaningful ways.

Richard Milligan

CONTENTS

ACKNOWLEDGMENTS

To my wife, Leah, you have been my greatest supporter. You believed in me when no one else did. Thank you for being willing to let me follow my dream by starting 4C Recruiting. The early days were hard, and only you would understand the difficulty of that season. Anyone I impact needs to know I couldn't do it without you. Thank you!

To my children Ethan, Gavin, Addi, and Haven, I am thankful that God gave you to me. Outside of your Mom, you are my greatest reason why I want to live true to my values. You give me a purpose way beyond myself which has allowed me to weather many difficult seasons in life. Thank you for that! May I inspire you to lead lives marked by generosity and impacting others. We are a world drowning in noise but starving for value. May you live a life marked by being valuable to others over yourself.

To my team at 4C Recruiting. When I said let's write a book, you all got as excited about it as I. Thank you for that! Most of the team played some supportive cast. Many of you simply picked up the slack so others could lean into the book project. Know I am thankful for each of you.

To those who played a specific role in the book, Chelsea, Chris, Mackenzie, Maddie, Madison, and Megan. Your insights, ideas, and creativity brought a lot of pieces to life!

To Adi, you took the chaos and made sense of the crazy. It wouldn't have been possible without you taking lead. Thank you!

To Rachel, Stephanie, and Tera, you connected the dots on ideas and stories through the written word in a way that will build aha's for leaders. You are all amazing talents in your own rights! Thank you for bringing this to life!

To Tim, the NFT project associated with this book wouldn't have been possible without you! Thank you!

How to Dominate Recruiting in a Digital World

FOREWARD
BY: RENÉ RODRIGUEZ

Welcome to the age of attention. Companies, politicians, ad firms, "influencers," and the media spend billions trying to capture our attention. Whether it be a swipe, a like, a purchase, a share, a referral, or a view, they are all fighting for it because where our attention goes, money flows. Period.

I have studied and watched this phenomenon for years, mostly from a position of frustration. I was frustrated because I came from an era where "content" truly was king. I spent tens of thousands of dollars to create high-quality videos that no one watched on social media. I couldn't understand it. They said content was everything, but why did I have such a hard time getting people to watch videos?

As frustrated as that made me, I was equally fascinated as to why my content wasn't gaining traction. So four years ago, I began my search for answers. Speaking with every successful social media person I could get in front of. Reading the books that claim to have THE "formula." Testing and trying a myriad of approaches, styles, and sequences. I learned very quickly that everyone had an opinion on what I should do, but no one could seem to get results. I also learned that this type of marketing was so new that there weren't any true "gurus." It was just too new and constantly changing. I thought the big brands would be the ones to follow and emulate, but I was sorely mistaken. What worked for the big brands did not work for the rest of us. I was feeling quite defeated.

I was sharing my frustration with my good friend Dave Savage, CEO of Mortgage Coach. He listened to me venting and complaining about how the world has changed and that people don't value good content anymore, blah, blah, blah. Basically, sounding like my parents saying how "back in their day...". He then calmly said, "I need to introduce you to my secret weapon. Richard Milligan of 4C." To be completely honest, I was not at all interested in taking the meeting but did so out of courtesy for my friend. After 5 minutes of meeting Richard, I felt like I had met a long-lost brother. A kindred spirit who understood the value of strategic planning, brand ethos, and good old-fashioned hard work. But he brought something I had not yet seen.

Richard understood this new, digital world, and he could articulate it in a way that made sense to me. He effortlessly connected the tried-and-true fundamentals of strategy along with the modern approaches to marketing and communications. He explained to me that the reason I wasn't getting traction was because I was communicating as if I had a captive audience. As a speaker, that's what we have, people in a room ready to listen to you. That was not the case in social media and should NOT be the strategy. He went on to explain why my strategy of emulating the bigger brand names would not work because I was not yet "known." When you are "known," people will watch what you have to say because they already have a connection with you and your content. He gave me the analogy that I must literally "audition" for people's attention with every single post, and that audition lasts only three seconds! It all began to make sense to me. I had to "stop the scroll"! In today's world, you can have all the solutions, the best information to share, and the strongest value proposition, but if you can't get people to stop scrolling so they can hear your message, you don't even exist.

Richard was the unicorn I had been searching for. Not only that, but his entire team was also just like him. They were smart, asked the right questions, dug in deep to understand my brand, and even uncovered elements I had been trying to articulate but couldn't find the words. They gave me a vision of what was possible and painted a picture that was attainable. I was hooked from the start.

This book could not have come at a better time. I would venture to guess that if you are reading these words, you, too, have felt some of the frustrations I have felt and are also looking for answers. I do have one frustration with Richard, and it's that he didn't write this book sooner.

I commend you for taking this journey and diving deep into what it takes to survive and thrive in this new world. So, grab your favorite pen, a new highlighter, and get ready to take notes. I promise you this: if you implement the strategies in this book, you will not only succeed but also dominate in this digital world.

René

va·lue gap

value gap

noun
The distance created by a leader with a strong core value system, marked by bringing value to people before asking for anything in return.

THE VALUE GAP

W hen it comes to the results Recruiting Leaders are getting, there is a growing distance between the top recruiters and those who are falling behind. I can immediately think of half a dozen Recruiting Leaders I coached in the past year that recruited teams of experienced top salespeople. These recruiters produced the equivalent size of companies that have been in business for 20, 30, and even 40+ years. And most of them did so without any corporate recruiting support!

When I bring this up, most leaders immediately want to know what specifically is being done to get those types of results. They want the easy shortcut, tactic, good phone script, or that secret text that will unlock the seemingly impassable door to such huge recruiting success.

They're looking for a short-term strategy that will lead to long-term success.

But, as you may have guessed by now—there's no "quick fix" for recruiting. None of those requested shortcuts or scripts make the top three list of important things that lead to these types of results. They probably don't even make the top ten list! The three key ingredients that lead to their major successes are:

1. Their ability to communicate their core vision, values, and why.

2. Their belief that in order to attract top talent, they must first lead by providing real value. A simple way to understand this is: "The more value you bring, the more in demand you become."

3. Their understanding of how to communicate these things in the digital world.

The first two of those key ingredients have always mattered—going back hundreds of years. Our new digital landscape now has created a need for the third. And that third ingredient creates a massive advantage in how many people can connect to a leader and have visibility into who they are without that leader having to sell themselves.

Those three things, when used together, create what I have defined as the "Value Gap," which gives Recruiting Leaders a massive advantage in the digital world.

A helpful way to look at it is through the understanding of reciprocity.

Reciprocity is simply: A relationship in which two people perform mutual actions based on the actions of the other.

Basically—people are social creatures. We mirror the behaviors and tasks that have already been modeled for us. It's a basic human trait. Think back to middle school. If another kid didn't invite you to their birthday party, you probably wouldn't invite them to yours either. On the other hand, once you've been to a friend's birthday, you feel like you should invite them to yours as well.

At that age, it's hardly even a conscious process. It's just what's "fair." We want to give others what they give to us. As we grow, and get a little more conscious of our social dealings, this process only increases. If someone sends us an encouraging email, then we want to be able to encourage them as well. We think something like, "Jared was so kind while I was struggling. I hope I can help him out too."

As leaders and recruiters, however, we need to know that we have to be the ones to start that chain of reciprocity. We have to be the ones to model the behavior, rather than the ones who wait and reciprocate! As Robert Cialdini put it, "Reciprocity is part of a healthy ongoing relationship. Nurture it by giving before asking for a request."

Basically, an effective Recruiting Leader understands that when they provide value and care to others, they are more likely to receive that value and care in return. When you give before asking for a request, people are more likely to want to give back.

re·ci·pr·oc·ity
law of reciprocity

noun

When you do something for someone, they want to do it for you as well. At the same time, it's much harder to ask someone else to do something that you've never done for them.

This leader likes my posts a lot. Because of the Law of Reciprocity, I want to engage more with their content

I remember reading Robert Cialdini's book "Influence: The Psychology of Persuasion" as a young 20-something salesperson.

His six principles of influence all left an impression on me, and acting on them led to early success not only in outside sales, but also in my life overall. Needless to say, I recommend the book!

Around the same time, I was also impacted by Brian Tracy's take on the "Law of Reciprocity." Simply put—give value and people feel inclined to give value in return. It's a human principle; it is how we have been hard-wired.

A Brian Tracy puts it, "Persuasion by reciprocation is based on the law of reciprocity. It's considered by many to be the most powerful law of human nature

A lot of Recruiting Leaders get this principle—it's pretty elementary human behavior, after all. But all too many haven't understood how to use the digital world as a way of accelerating the law of reciprocity. There is a disconnect when it comes to social media—they simply see these platforms as places to sell, sell, sell. Somewhere along the way, the early days of LinkedIn confused them into believing these platforms are places only meant to advertise "We are hiring!" in their news feeds. It also has them believing that there is a direct connection between sending right hooks into their prospects' DMs (Direct Messages) and expecting people to respond positively. But how often do you respond positively to an internet ad? Personally, I either ignore them or get outright annoyed by them.

The challenge is how much noise is created in the digital world. In 2007, the market research firm Yankelovich estimated that the average person saw up to 5,000 ads per day. Fast forward to 2022, and you will find most marketers agree that we see between 6,000 and 10,000 ads EVERY. SINGLE. DAY.

Let that sink in for a moment. Scroll through your social media, and you will find every two to three posts is a sponsored ad. The billboard sign is now digital, and it flashes something new every few seconds. I did this exercise myself. The page I just left on Google had 3 ads in the single view I was in. The article I read earlier on my phone had ads all over it.

If we join them by approaching social media like an ad campaign, we are just contributing to this noise—and will get drowned out right along with it.

THE BASIC TRUTH IS: PEOPLE ARE DROWNING IN NOISE BUT STARVING FOR VALUE.

This is where most Recruiting Leaders get stuck. They are tempted to throw up their hands, saying there is no value to be had in the digital world when it comes to recruiting. This, of course, would be a mistake. But as they say, you don't know what you don't know until you know something different.

A few months ago, I met with a Recruiting Leader—I mentioned him earlier, but let's go into more detail here. He came across my podcast (Recruiting Conversations) and asked to meet virtually. I said yes because I believe in bringing value before asking for value to be given, and over the course of an hour, I got to understand what he was trying to accomplish. In short, he had joined a new company that had a very lucrative model for anyone who could build teams. With each team he built, he would make passive income off of it. In his excitement, he went out and bought a lead list of 16,000 salespeople in his industry. He spent $8,000 doing so. He then thoughtfully laid out a game plan for spamming the heck out of the 16,000 people.

He didn't use the word spamming, but it's the only word I can think of for his methods. He was texting, emailing, and calling people over and over again, asking if they were "open to a better opportunity."

Now, remember what we've already said about "better." He wasn't really offering anything "different." He was essentially just promising the status quo.

At the time we connected, he was four months into his plan without much success. He had only hired several low producers who he was now wishing he hadn't hired. Needless to say, he was ridiculously frustrated. He believed it was his scripting that was causing a lack of results and wanted help changing it to something that would work.

There were two disconnects in his efforts.

1. He lacked a good core value system at the heart of his campaign.
2. He wasn't offering his contacts anything of value.

Ultimately, he missed the need to create a value gap.

His first disconnect: His only intentions were self-focused—build passive income, create freedom for himself. I asked him, "What's in it for the people you recruit?" His response lacked any real conviction that much value would be found in it for his recruits.

Where some people were forming their "vision, values, and why," his core value system came down to "me, myself, and I." It was wrapped up in him winning—end of story. I find this to be a common theme among leaders struggling to build teams.

The second disconnect: He had zero intentions of bringing anyone any real value. He wanted quick wins simply by inviting people to a lucrative income opportunity, should they be able to crack the growth code. This was ironic, considering he hadn't cracked it himself. He brought zero value.

Let me retract that statement—he brought *negative* value. He just added to the NOISE. Remember all those ads on your phone—ask yourself how many of them made you want to follow them. Anyone who adds to this noise risks not just being ignored but also being regarded with disgust. Is that the response you want from a recruit?

After an hour of discussing his goals, I gave him my best input. I said, "If you want to win in a big way, you must move to a heart posture of bringing value before you ask for value. The more value you bring, the more in demand you will become." Attractive Leaders who develop a better core value system look for ways to bring real and tangible value to people.

It was as though I was speaking a foreign language to him. He truly seemed confused by my thoughts around this. This would require him to engage in a thoughtful plan of pursuit, but he didn't seem to recognize the problem with his current, not very thoughtful plan.

This guy was acting as a hunter, and he didn't even realize how much all the noise he was making was scaring away his targets. He kept looking for the guaranteed "bait," shortcut, or secret method that would let him be successful without having to put in any real work.

I told him: Do some research, use better scripting, engage in a meaningful conversation, find out your prospect's big dream for where they want to go, and find out their greater why for what they are doing. Then, if you could help them accomplish their dream aligned with their why—pursue them with that.

One prerequisite I gave him was this: be committed to helping them accomplish their dream through the lens of their why "at all costs." This wasn't impossible, but I was asking him to scale what typically seems unscalable. He left the meeting with what I sensed was more frustration than when he arrived.

What he failed to connect was that recruiting done correctly is more like courtship—minus the romance part. Courtship is behavior designed to pursue someone, but the number one rule is that you have to show an interest in them. We've all been on a bad date with someone who only talked about themself and what they had to offer, without ever asking about who we are. Again, that's a bad date, and it's a bad way to treat anyone.

On the other hand, a genuine connection—romantic or not—is an incredibly affirming process. I was on a podcast a few years ago, and the host asked me what the biggest mistake being made by recruiters today was. My team turned my response into an eight-minute kinetic-style video that went viral. I discussed how we treat recruiting like a $29 widget sale when we should be courting our recruits.

Over the course of the past few years, I have seen again and again leaders have the kind of success that most don't believe is possible. And they do so in relatively short windows of time. Those leaders follow a digital blueprint that is the antithesis to approaching recruiting like a hunter. There are a number of things that contribute to these leaders' success, and those things are mostly tied to:

Value Creation and Affirmation.

When they connect with their recruits, they lead with real affirmation because they have used information available in the digital world to create meaningful conversations quickly. There is more information available today than ever in the history of the planet. And for a recruiter, this is great news. Information is helpful for warming up a relationship before we ever make contact over the phone.

For example: If you look me up on social media, here are a few quick points you will find...

I am family centered. My wife Leah and I have been married for twenty-four years and have four children and one grandson.

I love the outdoors.

I run several times a week.

I am crazy about recruiting and data around recruiting.

I host a podcast called Recruiting Conversations.

I love Jesus.

All of these make for conversation starters and are ways for someone to connect and immediately engage me.

In fact, I recently had a COO for a multi-billion dollar company reach out. The conversation started like this: "Richard, you don't know me but I feel like I know you. My CEO asked me to reach out as you have come up in a number of conversations at our company over the past year. We are looking for a Chief Strategy Officer and we believe that you have exactly what we are looking for. We have listened to your podcast, studied your content through social media, read your articles, and we love what you stand for with your values. We believe you are exactly the type of person who would bring a lot of value to our employees and company and help us grow. With that said, my CEO has asked if you would be willing to take his call so he could tell you more about this position."

Let me pause and say—this COO gets it! Of course, I am not going anywhere—nothing can pry me away from my calling here at 4C. But because he had done his research and led by affirming me, I took his CEO's call and connected with him. At that point, he had made me believe that even if I didn't take the role, I could gain some value from the meeting.

HOW I GOT STARTED

I pulled an all-nighter about 20 times in 2017. I worked probably another 200 nights that year where, after getting my kids to bed around 10:00 p.m., I came back

to my office and stayed up late, pounding away at my computer screen until 2:00 or 3:00 a.m. Anyone who's gone without sleep knows how that feels. Your head hurts, your stomach churns, and your whole headspace falls apart when you're exhausted. I was about 45 years old, way past the days when you could stay up all night without any repercussions.

So why was I doing this to myself? I had spent 15 years as a Recruiting Leader in the Mortgage Industry. I'd opened over 20 offices across the United States. I had a loving wife, amazing kids, and a wealth of personal friendships and business partnerships. I was, by most markers, successful—until I realized there was much more to do.

****

In my years of experience as a leader expected to recruit for my team, I discovered that recruiting coaching resources were severely lacking. Leaders were expected to recruit with little to no training. Best practices were often out-of-date hand-me-downs from a Google search. So when I first started my leadership journey, I sought every book, podcast, and every bit of information I could find to help me grow.

And I did grow. I opened office after office. But when I was offered a senior recruiting position, I knew it was time for me to leave that space and move on.

That experience showed me that I could step in and fill that void where the training was lacking.

There's a common phrase when we don't think a problem is important: "I wouldn't lose any sleep over it."

But once I recognized this problem, and my ability to do something to solve it, I realized something powerful.

I *would* lose sleep over this, because it is something that is *worth* losing sleep over.

The problem was this: there was—and still is—a severe lack of coaching or guidance for Recruiting Leaders.

Many still believed that recruiting was a mysterious and opaque field where "success" was more a measure of luck than skill. Many believed that recruiting wasn't important at all. The field had negative connotations associated with it, resulting in a negative interest in recruiting. The people most hurt by this lack of support were Recruiting Leaders. Many had been tossed into the position without any idea of what to do or how to do it. There was next to no training on how to recruit.

My experience had taught me that recruiting was a field, like any other, where you could learn tools to be more effective and successful.

To that end, I had decided to start 4C Recruiting, a company that would recognize the unique needs required of these leaders. We would work to train them in the principles of effective and compassionate recruiting and leadership. We would work to be a support for them in a field that was sorely lacking in support.

I believed it was a company that had value and would add value to people's lives. And for that, I was ready to lose some sleep.

At the time in 2017, I had one client. I had just one employee, too: myself.

We have grown from that humble beginning into a team of 40 people who devote their time to serving recruiting needs. We've gained skills and knowledge to help these leaders ideate their visions and connect more effectively with their teams and each other.

When I started 4C, on one of those sleepless nights, I made a long-term vision that by 2027, we would positively impact the lives of at least 10,000 Recruiting Leaders through our dedicated service.

Since 2017, we've made many steps towards that goal. We've helped leader after leader see greater success.

This book is another step in achieving that goal. We've identified another need and another way that we can help Recruiting Leaders.

Specifically, I'm talking about needs within the digital space.

Since my heyday as a Recruiting Leader, and even in the years since 2017, we have all seen major shift after major shift happening in the recruiting space. More and more, the digital world has become a vital aspect of how we recruit and how we lead. However, there is a severe lack of training for leaders in managing these systems and successfully recruiting using the powerful tools provided by digital and social media.

Throughout this book, we'll be providing exercises, evidence, tricks, hacks and case studies to help Recruiting Leaders see success in the digital world. We've also included a QR code at the end of the book to allow you access to even more resources. Our goal is that this book will provide Recruiting Leaders with concrete information and tips to help them navigate the ever-changing world of social media. The information compiled here represents a collective wealth of knowledge—my experience as a Recruiting Leader, along with the social media expertise and know-how of the 4C Team. The hope is that every reader of this book will represent another step toward our goal of helping 10,000 leaders to be more effective, valuable, and attractive to their teams and to top recruits.

It's like the title says:

We want to help you dominate recruiting in a digital world.

To that end, we'll start broad by answering two questions that may seem deceptively simple but are certain to be on the mind of many readers, recruiters, and others.

1. Why Does Recruiting Matter?

2. How Have Digital and Social Media Changed Recruiting?

The answers to these two questions will lead to a third:

3. Why Must Recruiting Leaders Humanize Themselves On Social Media?

I'm a doodler by nature. So during my coaching sessions, I often visualize ideas and principles through things like whiteboard drawings, stick people, and other charts and doodles. We'll be using a slightly cleaned-up version of these throughout this book to help keep things clear and help you "see" what we're doing here. Here's a quick example:

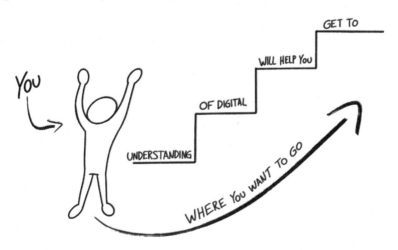

Now that we've stated our mission and purpose in sharing this information, we'll jump right into the first question.

QUESTION 1

WHY DOES RECRUITING MATTER?

Mini Exercise: Take a moment to write down two or three words that describe recruiting to you.

In my five or so years as a Recruiting Coach, I often ask people in my sessions to answer this question. So I'll ask the reader of this book to quickly follow the exercise as well, either on the notes app of your phone or in the space provided here. Write down maybe two words that you think describe "recruiting."

1.

2.

Whenever I ask this question, I see a lot of negative responses. I see words like "dishonest," "false narratives," "pushy," "stalking," and so on. There are many negative narratives associated with recruiting.

Where is this negative narrative coming from?

In order to start us all from a place of shared language and understanding, we will occasionally pause to provide definitions and explanations, such as the following:

What do we mean when we say "Recruiting Leader?"

According to the definition above, there are approximately 54,500 Recruiting Leaders in the mortgage industry alone (where I served). That's 54,500 branch managers, sales managers, market managers, area managers, regional managers, etc. That's anyone who leads a team and is in charge of recruiting for that team. There are also about 6,800 internal recruiters and 7,200 external recruiters in the industry. If we consider all the industries that exist outside of simply mortgages, there are

re·cru·it·ing
recruiting leader

proper noun

A leader who is managing a team and then is also responsible for recruiting to that team.

A Recruiting Leader in my field reached out with an exciting opportunity.

likely to be upwards of millions of Recruiting Leaders across the United States right now. A search for recruiters on LinkedIn alone brings up over two million results.

Immediately, when looking at these numbers, we're likely to think, "Wow, that's a lot of noise."

With that much noise, it's only natural that we have some negative connotations with recruiting. If every instrument in an orchestra started blaring at once, people would likely call that "noisy" too and feel negatively about it. On the other hand, a violin soloist playing well is something we'll immediately identify as music.

I'll go even further with this metaphor. An amateur playing the violin will only make screeches and noise. An expert is the one who will make something beautiful. Any of those instruments within the orchestra are capable of making a racket or making a song.

The negative connotations associated with recruiting are the result of focusing on the noise rather than the music. Still, with as many Recruiting Leaders as there are, it can be hard to cut through all that noise to find where the real magic is happening. So it's no surprise that many Recruiting Leaders don't even recognize themselves as such. Many people prefer to keep their title simply as "leader" and ignore their role's "recruiting" aspect. When we have negative connotations toward something, we tend to run away from it. We avoid the restaurant with bad reviews. We avoid the real estate agent with a bad reputation. We avoid the noise.

Our negative connotation toward recruiting is fairly weak. Ask anyone to explain why they think recruiting is "dishonest" or "stalkerish." They probably won't have a great answer. But that weak connotation is still enough to make many leaders avoid it. I hear this all the time in my coaching:

I don't really like to recruit.
Recruiting is hard.
I don't have time to recruit.

We'll be addressing these individual complaints some more, but they all come back to that negative perception of recruiting. So people don't want to run toward it because they think it's "bad."

Let's go back a moment, though. That very idea—that we avoid negative things and run toward positive things—is precisely why recruitment is such a powerful aspect of leadership. It's also why recruiting goes far beyond something as simple as "deceiving" someone.

The Great Resignation of 2021 taught us a lot. Here are some brief data points:

1. If their pay and purpose don't align, Millennials in particular (who will make up 75% of our workforce by 2025) are perfectly willing to walk.
2. 80% of job seekers say that an employer's reputation is important to them when choosing a job.

3. 90% of them are more likely to apply for a position with an organization that maintains its employer brand.

4. 1 in 3 people have rejected a job offer because of a bad online review.

What does this mean? It means that recruiting is about much more than its negative connotations. And it's about much more than just signing the most contracts and bringing in the most producers. It's about what I call "**Attractive Leadership.**"

at·tr·ac·ti·ve

attractive leader

proper noun

A leader who communicates what they believe, where they are going, and why they are committed to it so clearly that they magnetize people to their cause, idea, and team.

People avoid things or people that they feel negatively toward. But when people feel positively toward something or someone, they run toward it.

To put it simply, effective and meaningful recruitment means this: you want people to feel positively about you, the recruiter.

In practice, that's much more complicated. Attractive Leadership starts by drawing in talent who can contribute to your team and retaining them by helping them gain a sense of value and purpose as a member. This is why recruiting is so vital to leadership. Attractive Leadership, and its role in recruiting, is a matter of establishing your:

Vision
Values
Why

These are the core principles of what we call "Attractive Leadership." These ideas are where leadership and recruiting don't just overlap but inform each other. When you become a better recruiter, you become a better leader. Why? Because you can choose to attract and recruit top talent not by chasing them down but by drawing them in through your own strong principles and leadership.

When I started 4C, I defined them as the following.

Vision:

I wanted to create a company that would coach Recruiting Leaders and support them in both tangible and intangible ways as they embark on one of the most difficult aspects of leadership.

Values:
These are the core values that guide your team and how you run your business. One example I always used when building teams was this: *We treat each other better than our best friends.*

When I was a recruiter, I signed many top producers, only to find that they didn't align with the core values of the team I was trying to build within two or so years. In that case, I had to cut them from the team once they'd exhausted their chances for change. In other cases, people themselves chose to leave when they found that they didn't align with the spirit of what I was doing as a leader.

These principles allowed me to build teams that really did treat each other with respect, care, and genuine kindness.

This commitment to values and communication is exactly what recruitment is about. And these principles go way beyond the knee-jerk "negative" reactions we have when we hear the word "recruit."

These core values will be different for everyone. For me, a family environment in a team is important. But, it won't be important to everyone. We all have to choose our own principles in how we build a team.

It is vital to establish and codify your values early on. That way, you and your team can hold each other accountable to these values. When a team member does not stay true to this value—for instance, they gossip, send cruel emails when things go wrong, or otherwise fail to treat everyone *better than a best friend*—I know it's time to revisit the values I have previously shared with them.

Why:
When I started 4C, I asked myself: "Why would you do this if there wasn't a paycheck attached?"

Several motivators drive the things we do. These are divided into two categories: extrinsic motivators and intrinsic motivators.

Extrinsic motivators are easy to identify. These are things like money, titles, and other outer forces that drive us to desire achievement of the stereotypical markers of "success." In a way, these are the tip of the iceberg. In my coaching, I often see clients who feel worn down and uninspired in their career—and it's usually because only extrinsic motivators drove them. And once those extrinsic motivators have either been reached or run out, they have nothing left to light their fire. If money was all that was driving you, it's hard to know what to want once you make seven figures a year.

Intrinsic motivators are the bottom 90% of the iceberg.

They come from within us and can be much harder to see. But they also run much deeper. These are the guiding principles within our souls that drive us to do better and be more.

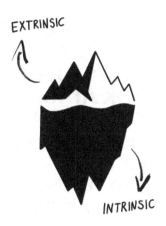

For instance, when I asked myself, "Why would you do this if there wasn't a paycheck attached," I realized that I didn't just want to be "successful," I wanted to be "useful" to the people I served. That deep desire I spoke of drove me to help leaders and my team become everything they want to be. These are values that stay with me through the great times and the difficult times alike. They're the kind of values that inspire a person to stay up all night to fix a problem or do more for others.

Finding Your Why:

Over the past five years of coaching more than 1,200 Recruiting Leaders, I have come to this conclusion: *few leaders are truly passionate about what they do.*

I have seen the disconnect that stems from having no vision for where they are going, no clarity around their core values, and no understanding of the *intrinsic why* for what they do for work.

People connect to people. They connect to someone who establishes their vision (what they will do), their values (how they plan to do it), and their "why" (what drives them to do this).

When I started 4C Recruiting, I sat down and created a document called "Why I Do What I Do." Nowadays, our whole team calls it "Why We Do What We Do."

Every day, I'm happy that I had the foresight to create this document to serve as a guidepost for *why* I stayed up all those nights, *why* we're all here, and *why* we are so committed to our work and to each other. It helps us see our trouble and treasure clearly and reminds us that the treasure is always greater than the trouble.

A SLEEPLESS NIGHT WAS WORTH IT FOR ME, BECAUSE I COULD LOOK AT THIS DOCUMENT AND UNDERSTAND THAT THE TROUBLE WOULD LEAD TO THE TREASURE I HAD LAID OUT.

This document is part of what Attractive Leadership is all about. The Attractive Leader doesn't chase people down. Instead, they draw people to them through a genuine connection to these principles.

To that end, here's another exercise. I don't want to build it up too much, but this may be one of the most important exercises of your career.

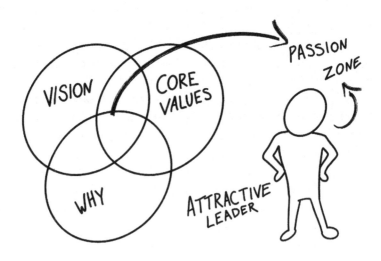

EXERCISE: CREATING YOUR "WHY I RECRUIT" DOCUMENT

Here, in your notes app, or wherever, write down why you're doing *this,* all of this, this whole "leadership" thing and "recruiting" thing. Take it seriously, and take yourself seriously. We want this document to be the start of something that you can refer back to when you're struggling along the path to becoming a better recruiter and leader. It will be your guidepost and connection to yourself and your passions. At the end of this chapter, I'll share 4C's "Why We Do What We Do," in case it's helpful as a model to find your own why.

Richard Milligan

WHY I RECRUIT:

WHAT IS THE REWARD (TREASURE) THAT YOU WILL GET FROM RECRUITING?

Richard Milligan

WHAT IS THE TROUBLE YOU WILL HAVE WHEN RECRUITING?

WHAT ARE YOU GOING TO CONTRIBUTE? WHAT ARE YOU GOING TO SAY "YES" TO AND WHAT ARE YOU GOING TO SAY "NO" TO?

4C'S WHY WE DO WHAT WE DO

We believe Recruiting Leaders have the most challenging position in any business and deserve the training necessary to succeed in their role as a leader who also recruits.

These are the best people in any industry. They work tirelessly at their own emotional, physical, and time expenses to serve their people.

Recruiting and leading are intertwined; thus, when we teach someone how to become a great recruiter, they, in turn, become a better leader.

There is an intersection where leading and recruiting overlap. It is called Attractive Leadership. When we teach Attractive Leadership (the importance of vision, core values, and why), it impacts people under the Recruiting Leaders' care for the better.

We do this because we love people, and people matter to us.
We do this because we empathize with the Recruiting Leaders' struggle.

We do this because great leaders influence things outside the walls of their business leadership.
We do this because we believe that one change changes everything.

We do this because God has equipped us, inspired us, and led us to this place.

This is why we here at 4C Recruiting do what we do! It is more than a job or a career! It is our calling!

Remember that this is a model. We all have our own drivers, our own values, and our own why. These principles are unique to every leader, and that specificity and uniqueness will make you attractive to recruits.

Now that we've established what recruiting is all about and what the Attractive Leader is, we'll leap into our next question—after a quick success story. Throughout the book, we'll share stories of leaders who have seen success on social media by doubling down on content aligned with their vision, values, and why. We hope their example will serve as inspiration!

Richard Milligan

CASE STUDY:
JEFF RICHMOND & LEXY SANCHEZ

J eff Richmond and Lexy Sanchez aren't just business partners—they are life partners as well.

The company they work for, ExP Realty, LLC, was ranked as one of the top 4 brokerages nationwide in 2022. In addition, they are a pair of top-ranked real estate agents and Team Growth Leaders.

With her two master's degrees in organizational development and public administration, Lexy was one of the top 1% of real estate producers in the nation and has become a respected leader in the real estate industry. She personally developed a non-profit arm of ExP Realty, "Extend a Hand," which helps agents in need.

Jeff, meanwhile, has a doctorate in jazz music. Before working in real estate, he was a college professor and musician who performed worldwide. When he broke into real estate, he built a team and quickly saw success.

Nowadays, Jeff and Lexy are both growth leaders for "The Community," a unique service that provides tools and coaching for real estate professionals.

Part of what makes these two interesting as a success story is that they essentially have had to build three brands: Lexy's personal brand, Jeff's personal brand, and the personal brand of the two as a collective team. They share about their travels together, their experiences with coaching, and their relationship at home and in business. The fact that they've been able to build such a level of influence is a testament to the impact social media has on Attractive Leadership.

What can we learn from Jeff and Lexy? One interesting insight they shared was that they've managed to preserve a certain level of privacy online. "We try to strike a healthy balance of representing our true selves while also preserving privacy and our most intimate moments. Sometimes not telling the whole story says more than being omnipresent on social media channels."

Many leaders struggle with finding the right balance between private and public as they build their personal brands. Of course, that doesn't necessarily mean hiding too much of yourself or trying to be "fake." It's possible to draw a personal boundary between what you do or don't feel comfortable sharing online while maintaining a consistent and authentic presence.

Jeff and Lexy still share plenty, but they focus more on being "real" than anything scripted or overpowering. "The best content we post is pictures of our faces. We are real people and we always want that to be at the forefront of our messaging . . . Ironically, we know digital marketing inside and out, but we've placed much more long-term emphasis on building relationship capital than posting about our company. That stuff tends to just get lost in the shuffle. Keeping it real has served us well in regards to who is in our life—business especially. When people see us online and then get to know us, they feel assured they know the real Jeff and Lexy. We love that and will never change that for hopes of more likes or shares."

Keep in mind that you'll never be able to build a strong, authentic presence online without *ever* making yourself vulnerable. Vulnerability is a powerful connector and model. However, it's easy to overthink authenticity. Jeff and Lexy said it well: "Being 'authentic' has become a term that is tossed around casually by people now. We believe in authenticity as a core value, but we also don't believe that authenticity is something that should require a ton of thought, creativity, or anything else. If you're spending hours trying to figure out how to be more authentic, you've failed to comprehend the definition of that word."

When we live our lives being thoughtful and focused on the world around us, we often wind up with tons of stories, pictures, and other content to share. This natural content will automatically be more authentic—given that it comes from our authentic lives—without stressing too much about what authenticity even "means." Again, Jeff and Lexy sum it up very well: "We choose to live real moments of inspiration, not by algorithmic demands."

Part of the success they've seen is due to treating social media as a place to share their lives rather than a place to obsess over their business. "In terms of direct recruiting, we do not use paid ads, direct messaging, or any spam techniques to push content because they don't help us to build our relationships. We tend to be much more relational—phone, face to face, etc. Social media creates confirmation that our life is characterized by the freedom and love we believe in and truly live out every day."

Much of this book focuses on the principle of "like attracts like." Basically, if you post according to your "why" and your values, you'll attract people who align with those values.

This bond will be much more powerful than something as simple as money.

Jeff and Lexy make another compelling argument along those lines. "We are definitely turned off by people using social media to decidedly promote an agenda in a sneaky way. Gaming the system or looking for shortcuts says a lot about people, but also, people see right through it. You have to realize that you want to work with smart people—and smart people can sniff out BS without much effort. So, trying to figure out how to trick, game, or deceive people really only pushes your optimal leads away. Focusing our efforts on what truly matters to us ultimately attracts the type of people we want to partner with in business and life. Eliminating falsehoods keeps us true to our ethos while also sorting out the wrong associations."

Ultimately, BS will only attract BS. Genuine content connects more with mart people precisely because they can see through anything that's too fake or contrived. And we all, hopefully, want smart and genuine people to be the ones connecting with us.

For Jeff and Lexy, part of building their personal brand meant creating something positive. "We don't post negative things very often, if at all. We really believe that social media is an opportunity to stand out in a world full of negative complaining. We don't live that way personally and don't want our social channels to be negative like the news tends to be. We stay optimistic, positive, and inspired because it's true to us. Life is too fantastic to focus on the negatives. Ironically, sometimes posting on social media reminds us of that!"

In 2012, Facebook did a secret study where they changed people's News Feeds. They showed one group content with more positive words and stories and gave the others almost nothing but negative content. At the end of the week, the people who viewed positive content were more likely to post positively. Conversely, those who saw negative content were more likely to post negatively.

This emphasis on positivity is significant because we typically want people to feel positive about us. Posting authentic, real, and constructive content will result in a feedback loop in which audiences feel positively about you. It's important to remember that "being positive" doesn't necessarily mean being fake" either. Jeff and Lexy made the powerful choice to share content with a positive tone, so they could "stand out in a world of negative complaining." Many people are not particularly constructive on social media. And there *is* a place for some negativity. For instance, when you gain insight from a moment of failure, know that authentically sharing will have a powerful impact on your audience and how they view you.

Our values, typically, represent the things we love. Making content that aligns with those values will naturally result in content that feels more constructive and positive. Producing content that only focuses on the things we dislike means ignoring our values. So you end up with content that's only about the things we don't care for or value. That's a very negative way to post, and audiences will respond to that negativity.

"We'd rather focus on the elements of life that actually matter: relationships, love, truth, trust, honor, contribution, impact, and making a difference to anyone and everyone that comes in contact with us or our content. It's possible this has delivered less quantity, but it has definitely delivered more quality and tends to reinforce our life philosophy."

–Jeff and Lexy

di·gi·t·al
digital

adjective or noun

Technology in modern-day society.

*More and more, businesses are existing within
a digital landscape.*

QUESTION 2:
HOW HAVE DIGITAL AND SOCIAL MEDIA CHANGED RECRUITING?

I n 2003, social media took off in a big way. LinkedIn and Facebook (known as "FaceMash" in the early days) were both founded. Suddenly, people had these structures built around connecting with others online– even continents away.

That change was massive enough on its own. But those structures have only continued to evolve and adapt over the last 15 years: the rise of Twitter and Instagram have also drastically altered the social media landscape.

Jump to 2020, when COVID-19 became a worldwide pandemic and changed just about everything—especially how we conducted business. We saw an accelerated shift into this new digital age with virtual meetings, Zoom, etc. Now, more than ever, connecting through technology and social media is vital to success.

However, as digital has changed how we interact with one another, many recruiters have failed to recognize the opportunities in this major shift as it's taken place.

Most people see social media as having made businesses less personal. And in many ways, this is true. Businesses *have* become less personal because it's hard to connect to an intangible entity like a company. Because of this, template-style posts and other generic content abound on corporate social media accounts.

But some leaders and recruiters have come to recognize social media for what it can be: a recruiting "super weapon."

Growing up, I played a lot of Mario Brothers (let's not even get into how much video games have changed since those days). Anyone who played the game knew about cheat codes. You could input these codes into the console to give you advantages when playing the game.

One example is that you could get extra lives for your character—if you died, you could come back more times.

Another example was that you could give your character the ability to do a "mega-jump" from a standing still position.

Social media is like a cheat code for recruiting. It gives you more life on the system and more staying power. It lets you go from standing still straight to leaping forward and gaining new ground.

Don't just take my word (or Mario's) for it.

- 86% of job searchers in 2022 used social media in their job search.

- 65% of people are open to hearing about a job opportunity from a personal connection on social media.

It's that powerful, yet it's criminally underutilized by Recruiting Leaders. This is especially disappointing when we consider how powerful social media can be for the Attractive Leader.

But what should a Recruiting Leader do to attract recruits on social media? Is it enough just to post a lot about company culture and values?

Our belief at 4C is that people connect with people. Humans are social creatures, and we want to see other humans

Social media content has 561% more reach when employees share content versus when a company shares. In addition, content from employees is typically shared 24 times more frequently than company content.

People connect to people, not to companies.

I'll share this vital piece of advice for the Recruiting Leader on Social Media.

YOU ARE YOUR MOST VALUABLE PRODUCT.

Eighty-two percent of people are more likely to trust a company when senior executives are active on social media. Seventy-seven percent of people say they are more likely to buy when the CEO of the business uses social media.

The leaders of your company are your product.

I'll say it again: your CEO, your C-Suite, your executive leaders, and your managers should be on social media. All of these people are capable of achieving more reach on an individual level than their company does on a corporate level.

I mentioned earlier that it's estimated by 2025, millennials will make up 75% of the workforce.

Millennials are one of the most educated and qualified workforces in American history. Sixty-one percent of them have attended college. They're looking for opportunities to grow, and they're looking for opportunities to align with the right companies. Because of this, they're not afraid to job hop in the search for the right culture to fit their needs. As a result, many of them move companies every three years.

The millennial workforce consists of people born between the early 80s and mid-90s. These are people who grew up while social media was coming up. They've been there for all of its changes. So they're comfortable with using it as a tool to connect. Seventy-three percent of millennials used social media in their last job search.

Leverage social media to show people on the "outside" an idea of what it's like on the "inside." And you want the "inside" to look not just good—but *human.*

And keep this in mind: Eighty-two percent of people say they would quit their job if they had a bad manager.

Leadership is a vital aspect of why someone would choose a position or company. To put it in the simplest terms: nobody wants to sign on to a job where they believe that leadership is bad. Everybody wants a job where they believe leadership will be good.

People want to feel connected to and be heard by their leadership. And people connect more to individuals than to companies.

So the question is: how do your leaders look on social media? Do they look like human, caring people?

Or do they just look like one headshot and the company logo? The more relatable we are, the more loyalty we'll earn. So let's look at Gavin's story to see the importance of authenticity.

CASE STUDY:
GAVIN EKSTROM

G avin Ekstrom has been in the mortgage industry for over 30 years now. Currently, his time is dedicated to his passion– coaching– and his wife and six kids.

With such a long career, Gavin was there for the rise of social media from the very beginning. But, where many choose to dismiss its possibilities, he doubled down, increased his personal brand, and became an Attractive leader online.

His advice? "I have found that it's okay to be vulnerable. It took some time, and I still fight it. Still, my belief is that recruits will move towards leaders they can trust."

The relationship between vulnerability and trust is powerful. According to Jeff Polzer, a professor of organizational behavior at Harvard, vulnerability is "...about sending a really clear signal that you have weaknesses, that you could use help. And if that behavior becomes a model for others, then you can set the insecurities aside and get to work, start to trust each other and help each other."

This concept applies to recruiting as well. If we are vulnerable on social media, then our followers—and potential recruits—will see that behavior modeled and feel comfortable being vulnerable as well. So often, we underestimate just how much someone has to put themself at risk, so to speak, when they reach out and ask for a job!

According to Gavin, part of his success is also due to sharing stories about his work and business. "...in this market I also feel recruits want a player coach. Someone who is still in the game."

At the very least, recruits want to see evidence that you understand what they're going through and are on their side. Sharing those direct experiences builds camaraderie and connection. The task of being vulnerable is not easy but the rewards are definitely worth the pain. As Gavin puts it, "It has provided me the opportunity to increase my reach. Before, I was only focused mainly in the Colorado market. ...we now are being seen globally. It also has allowed potential recruits to see who I am as a husband, father, leader, and coach. Even when it might not be the most comfortable, this gives them the feeling of connection. In some situations, they know more about me than I do them!"

Gavin has shared one of the most important insights of building your brand online—you must make yourself known if you want others to let you get to know them. You have to model the behavior you want to see from recruits, team members, or anyone online. If you want them to be vulnerable with you, you have to take that first step. But if you do, your radius of Attractive Leadership will become larger, stronger, and more honest than ever.

QUESTION 3:
WHY MUST RECRUITING LEADERS HUMANIZE THEMSELVES ON SOCIAL MEDIA?

Millennials are looking to social media for career shifts. They, like most people, want to work for a leader that will treat them well and act like a human to them.

Therefore, **leaders need to humanize themselves on social media.**

Doing this isn't always an easy task. Many people struggle with being vulnerable to social media, especially in a professional setting.

But we're all people. We all understand failure, family, and frustration. So we connect far better with these human, unscripted moments than we ever will with a social media template or a brand logo.

> **"**
> **LEADERS NEED TO HUMANIZE THEMSELVES ON SOCIAL MEDIA.**
> **"**

You humanize leadership by establishing a social media presence that represents your vision, values, and why. Doing this allows those on the outside to see what things are like on the inside. The objective is to show people that your company is full of people who connect with and care for their teams.

Here's something that I want us to understand as well. There are two kinds of opportunities that exist when job hunting.

There's the **Better Opportunity** and the **Different Opportunity**.

The Better Opportunity is something a lot of recruiters lean on. They say, "We're a little bit better than that other company. We sell more, we make more, we do something better." These tactics are common in email blasts, text message campaigns, and so on.

The Different Opportunity, though, represents something new entirely. It represents a brand new opportunity that doesn't exist anywhere else. As Sally Hogshead put it in her book *Fascinate*: "Different is better than better."

A Dynamic Leader is someone who isn't afraid to use their cheat codes to empower themselves to be human on social media. As a result, they can showcase not just how they're better—but also how they're different.

Every company makes money. Some make more; some make less.

But your personal leadership brand doesn't exist anywhere else. Your core vision, values, and why all represent something that's not just "better," but is radically and attractively different from what the competition can offer.

OFFERS CAN BE MATCHED.
YOU CANNOT.

I often refer to the BAM Zone. This stands for:

BELONGING, AFFIRMATION AND MEANING.

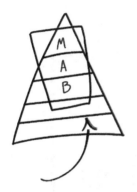

I based this on Maslow's hierarchy of needs. According to this hierarchy, the lowest motivator is food and shelter. Once we have these, we can start seeking self-actualization.

What does this mean? Once people feel secure in their finances, they'll start looking for the next step. They won't be looking for *more* money, or *more* security. Instead, they'll be looking for the things that matter to help them feel self-actualized. That means the BAM zone.

You can offer these things to people who are already high achievers. You can offer them something radically new— Belonging, Affirmation, and greater Meaning.

You become the system's cheat code if you showcase how you're different. Then, you can attract talent from a distance. Your personal brand becomes a beacon that reaches out and draws people toward you. And not just any people—you'll attract the most talented, educated, dynamic, qualified people. These are the people who see you doing something different. It's attractive, so they want to be a part of that.

Keep this in mind as well: people respond and connect more with stories than with data. Again—they connect more with people than with companies.

Recently I was brought in to consult for a marketing department at a major company. The department was seeing negative growth. I highlighted the need for them to build a marketing framework that would elevate their leaders.

Why? Because leaders are the product, and you need to market that product. People on the marketing side need to listen here: build frameworks and teams within your department to enable leaders to create personal digital content. Leaders need to feel empowered by their companies to develop their personal brands.

Give them the capacity to talk about their life as a mother.

Give them space online to discuss what happened during the team meeting.

Give them a chance to let people on the Outside see what it's like on the Inside.

Don't let Glassdoor reviews be their only view Inside the company. Companies represent the outer layer facade of culture and brand. However, people are what exist on the Inside. And that's what job seekers genuinely want to know about. Here are two stories that serve as an example of this principle.

GEORGE'S STORY:

I had a coaching client, who we'll call George, who had purchased a list of 16,000+ top salespeople in their field.

He had built an intense recruiting campaign. It was a text messaging campaign, an email campaign, a dialer campaign, and a social media messaging campaign. He covered all his bases.

But everything he talked about was purely predicated on "selling, selling, selling." "We're a better company. We have better tools. We have better systems. We sell more."

They were better, not different. And George didn't see much success when he played the numbers game.

The only thing he was successful in was validating a working unsubscribe button.

ANNE'S STORY:

A 4C client, a Recruiting Leader we'll call Anne, had sent an offer to a top recruit in her field. She continued to reach out for about ninety days, trying to convince them to sign. The recruit went stagnant at some point. And realistically, they were probably getting a lot of offers—this was a top 1% salesperson, after all.

But then, one Monday, Anne made a LinkedIn post about a personal experience she'd had with leadership.

Later that day, she got a text message from that recruit. Basically, it said: *I read your Monday morning post. I'm ready to sign. You're the type of leader I want to align with moving forward.*

An Attractive Leader can convert people because they introduce something new and different. They introduce values—which are more important to us than money.

"Better" doesn't make people feel dissatisfied with what they have. An email campaign promising "more" won't get people to sign.

"Different" does. Values inspire someone to make the leap and trust in a leader who is doing something they want to be a part of.

Social media is how we show that we're different. It's how we send out the beacon and become hacks in the system. Its reach is powerful, but its ability to connect us with people who align with our principles as Attractive Leaders is a powerful tool. A strong social media presence and leadership brand are not just options for an effective Recruiting Leader—they're a requirement.

CASE STUDY:
JOHN LEGERE

U nfortunately, many of us leaders cut our teeth in a world that was sales, sales, sales. We memorized our scripts, got our pitches down pat, and learned how to get into a "sales" mindset. That method might work when you're talking in one-on-one meetings, but in the global marketplace of social media—it couldn't be deadlier.

According to social media consultant Paul Gillin, as quoted in Forbes: "Companies are tuned toward delivering messages, but that doesn't work in social media channels...customers don't go to social media sites to get advertising messages." He warns that the more a company tries to sell via social media, the more likely people will just stop listening.

RADICAL CHANGE REQUIRES A REVOLUTIONARY MODEL

The shift to seeing success on social media requires a radical change in how you engage. We've provided ample evidence and advice for the benefits of Attractive Leadership—radical change requires a revolutionary model.

Because it's often easier to understand the principles and benefits of building your personal brand on social media when we see them play out in real-time, I've included the following case study as an illustrative exercise in the power a single leader can hold on social media:

About how much time per day do you spend on your cell phone?

The short answer is probably "a lot," but I don't ask the question to shame anyone. Increasingly, these tiny, mind-boggling machines assist us in our daily lives. As a result, we've all likely considered and researched the wireless network that will support these phones. So we explore the best deals, which gives the most data, what plan will best support our family, and everything else.

Now here's another question. Do you think you would recognize the CEO of your wireless company if you saw them at the coffee shop tomorrow?

The short answer is probably "No," unless you happen to know them personally. To the average person on the street, these CEOs are a mystery. Many of them aren't even on Twitter.

None of these people have made a particular effort to *be recognizable.* When you head a brand as huge as a company such as Verizon Wireless, you don't necessarily need to worry about your personal branding or social media presence.

Or so you might think.

I followed John Legere on Twitter in 2015, along with 1.3 million other people.

Granted, I had worked for T-Mobile as a B2B sales manager back in my twenties. They'd been great to work for, enough that even ten years after leaving, I was keeping an eye on the company's doings.

When they brought in Legere as CEO, he was known, in rather niche circles, for his ability to bring companies back from the brink. He'd saved Asia Global Crossing, a troubled fiber optic networking company. When they first brought him on, he put the company in bankruptcy protection. After ten years of his careful rebuilding, they were bought for 1.9 billion.

Still, when he became the CEO of T-Mobile, he was far from a household name.

He would be soon. In fact, he would quickly rebrand himself to the point that he was probably the single wireless CEO that anyone would recognize if they saw him in the coffee shop.

And he became famous precisely by following none of the "rules" for how the CEO of a major wireless company was expected to act.

Legere was brought on as CEO of T-Mobile in September of 2012. By the end of 2013, its number of social media followers had almost doubled. The social media analytics site Socialbackers (now "Emplifi") ranked T-Mobile as a "Top-10 Socially Devoted Company."

The company as a whole was doubling down on social media engagement under Legere's orders, and Legere himself was leading the charge.

"The change at T-Mobile needed to start with me," he said. "I knew I needed to go all the way in order to change the culture to something that reflected who we were, or would be, as a company."

He changed himself to reflect this new culture. "I grew out my hair, swapped out the suit and tie for a leather jacket and a magenta T-shirt, and threw away the filter," he said.

By "throwing away the filter," he was referring to the outdated ideas of professionalism that existed at the time, particularly for wireless CEOs: wear a suit, only talk about the brand, and "Don't rock the boat." This unspoken filter is likely partly why so few wireless CEOs are particularly visible.

Legere, instead, swore often and called out his competition directly. He called Verizon and AT&T "Dumb and Dumber." He wasn't just active on social media– he was brazen.

He was also, vitally, very *human*.

He became particularly famous for "Slow-Cooker Sundays," a weekly segment that ran for two years. He would log onto Facebook Live and share a favorite slow-cooker recipe from that week.

What's more human than a set-it-and-forget-it tool like a slow-cooker? It's hardly glamorous, and yet those streams, at their height, saw over a million viewers.

He joined Twitter in May of 2013. By March 2016, he had over two million followers and sent over 17,500 tweets. 2016 was the same year Twitter gave him his own bespoke emoji that appeared when anyone used the hashtag "#TweetJohn." For the record, this was only the second emoji Twitter ever made dedicated to a specific person– the first was of Pope Francis.

It's easy to ask, "What exactly does *his* story have to do with *my* cell service?" Really, the answer is "Everything."

T-Mobile had been struggling when they brought on Legere. The year before he joined, they'd lost 4.3 billion dollars. In addition, they were struggling to compete with the big wireless companies like AT&T and Verizon.

At the start of his tenure, Legere sat with the help-line call centers at T-Mobile and listened to the actual problems that people were having with their service. He closely followed the hashtags on Twitter. And he discovered what people were actually bothered by when they complained about their wireless service. "I have a much more precise pulse on what's happening, even with individual customers," Legere said.

The results inspired Legere. He immediately began to break the rules, not just for how a CEO should act, but for how a wireless company should operate.

He rebranded T-Mobile as the "un-carrier," directly pitting them against the other companies and their outdated policies. He led the removal of long-term contracts and global roaming charges at a time when that was unheard of. T-Mobile began paying other carriers' termination fees to encourage people to switch. Nowadays, we recognize many of his practices as standard, given how the other wireless carriers quickly followed suit. He adopted a new, bright color for T-Mobile—magenta—to match their new exciting policies.

And while he did all of this, he made himself very visible on social media.

He live-streamed his jogs around New York.

He wore a Batman mask to events.

He often called out the competition directly, once tweeting,

"Raise your hand if you have ever been personally victimized by @VerizonWireless #NationalMeanGirlsDay."

He was the CEO king of social media in a time when few in the business world were engaging much with the medium at all.

At a GeekWire Summit in 2014, Legere stated: "The truth is, I learn almost everything I need to know to run T-Mobile in there." His reference to "there" being Twitter. He went on to say, "I take every Tweet that comes in and I read it. I forward it to people. My executive team gets them, we reply, and at my staff meeting every Tuesday, we track social media impressions, what they are and how we've responded to them. It takes a ton of time, and it's a lot of fun. You got to be real, and you got to be out there. But I am having a ball with it."

While Legere became recognizable very quickly as he grew his personal brand, none of this would have been enough on its own to build the company back up. But Legere was using his personal branding as a supplement to new company branding. The new, crazy CEO was adopting some new crazy policies.

During slow-cooker Sundays, Legere often encouraged people to switch to T-Mobile with his characteristic candor. And they did. People were paying attention.

It's fair to say that Legere was polarizing. In communication, polarizing has a push-pull effect. It repels those who disagree with you and pulls those who agree with you. Legere's behavior may have pushed some away (Buzzfeed called his promoted tweets one of the most "annoying" ad campaigns in history), but it pulled many others closer. He came on in 2012, and by 2015, after consistent effort on and off social media, T-Mobile's revenues increased by 15%. Shares shot up more than 400% between 2013 and Legere's resignation in 2020. They saw growth at a rate twice as fast as AT&T's and seven times as fast as Verizon's. This is particularly stunning when we consider that, in 2015, T-Mobile invested the least capital of any of the major wireless carriers at the time by a huge degree.

The wireless industry is an expensive one when it comes to capital. It costs a lot to keep a network running and up-to-date with new trends. In 2015, 4G became a hot commodity, for instance, but that doesn't happen without a company investing.

In 2015, Verizon invested 11.7 billion dollars.

AT&T invested 8.9 billion.

Sprint invested 6 billion.

And T-Mobile invested 4.7 billion, the smallest amount by far.

There was simply no way that T-Mobile could compete with the other wireless companies when it came to capital investment—especially the top two competitors. As seen by AT&T investing close to double what T-Mobile did that year, and Verizon investing close to triple.

Competing in that field was a non-starter. And yet, T-Mobile saw the most growth in 2015 by far. By the end of the year, they had edged out Sprint to become the number three wireless carrier on the market.

T-Mobile's growth only continued. In 2016, they led the industry in customer growth, seeing 8.2 million new customers.

They also saw incredible financial growth in 2016: 37.2 billion dollars in total revenue.

What do these numbers show us?

It would take a huge stretch of the imagination to think that any of this growth existed in a vacuum. While T-Mobile could never compete when it came to capital, Legere had found the niche where they could not only compete but *dominate*: social media.

Legere was very frank about this. He had quickly carved out a space and a following for himself on social media. And he knew other CEOs would never be able to imitate him: "The reason I know they won't be able to take advantage of what I do is that there's no f––ing way they're going to be able to spend their day doing what I do...I wake up in bed, and I do Twitter for an hour and a half just to catch up." He once estimated that he spent around 7 hours a day on social media.

Obviously, all of this effort was a major driver of the company's growth under Legere's leadership. The increased social media presence drew attention to T-Mobile's status as the "Un-carrier," or the wireless company that was going to "undo" all the policies that frustrated people about their wireless service. These policies **attracted** David Carey, who'd worked with Legere at Global Crossing, to join him at T-Mobile as an executive vice president. He and Legere both recognized that the company needed to transform. "We had 50,000 employees with an average age of 28. We can't come in like a bunch of fuddy duddies."

They implemented other policies to embrace their employees and encourage team growth and retention. Legere was once asked who his role model was. He responded, "Truthfully, without being cliche: the reps and front line (people) in the care centers." The fact that he had sat with these people at their jobs made this comment ring as true and heartfelt—certainly more true than it might have felt coming from many other CEOs at the time.

There was also the fact that, when T-Mobile's merger with MetroPCS in 201 went public, Legere insisted every employee get founder stock.

When Deutsche Telekom objected, Legere insisted. As he put it, "I need ever single one of these employees to be owners, not renters." He won thi negotiation because he insisted on it.

Here, we see someone showing the Outside what it's like to be on the Inside with an Attractive Leader. It's a place where the CEO has actually listened to the angry phone calls you field every day and is passionate about changing the company in ways that will radically change your work life.

What is there to learn from Legere?

In simple terms—he was funny, weird, and *human* at a time when very few CEOs were bothering to even be visible. He made himself reachable and connectible. He recognized the power social media had to build connections and attract people.

The CEO of AT&T didn't even have a Twitter at the time. Many CEOs still don't have one now, seven years later. But Legere's consistent presence and humanity—both on and off social media led to a decade-long rise of T-Mobile. In late 2018, Legere had 132,000 mentions on social media in one month. Those mentions came from more than 58,000 unique authors of posts.

"The benefit I have with social? There is no way that my peer CEOs are going to do this. There's absolutely no way. I sit at the restaurant, at the bar with my phone down, typing away. I lay in bed at night for two hours, an hour, and I wake up, and I am hitting the keys. There's no way these country club-running guys are going to do it. Not to mention what comes in. But it's a competitive advantage and I think it's worth billions. Billions."

This section isn't here to "shill" for T-Mobile. Instead, it's to "shill" for the idea of creating a consistent and humanizing presence on social media.

It's difficult for many of us to dominate in our respective industries—we can't all invest as much money as the big guys, and we don't all have access to the same resources. But we do all have the same level of access to social media. We just have to *choose* to invest enough time and effort into making a presence that represents our values and our company. Social media's competitive advantage becomes even more real and powerful, particularly when we choose to incentivize this effort at a company level. You can't always offer the cheapest price, and you can't always dominate when it comes to money, but you can dominate in the social media sphere. If you choose to double down on your leadership brand and social media presence, you will also reap the benefits of Attractive Leadership. John Legere recognized this—he wasn't just competitive—he became the "best" and most valuable regarding his company's social media presence. This concept worked for a wireless CEO, and it can work for any one of us, no matter how small or huge our role may be.

FOLLOW-UP QUESTIONS:

1 Legere made a name for himself through slow-cooker recipes, of all things. So what's something you're passionate about that, while not strictly "professional," could add value to the lives of the people who follow you?

2 Legere drew attention by being unafraid to be himself—to be 100% authentic. This tactic played out in his language choices. Some would have called him unprofessional, but they were 100% Legere. I call these "isms." An ism is a phrase or statement you regularly use in conversations. For example, one "Richard-ism" is replacing the term "recruiting" with "relationship building." Several others I commonly use are "Attractive Leadership," "Recruiting Leader," and "Surrogate Leader." Use this space to brainstorm some of your personal "voice." What are some slang terms, common phrases, or otherwise "unprofessional" terms that you use every day? Do you have any favorite sayings or idioms? Maybe ask a friend or spouse to help you identify personal catchphrases or expressions that you use often!

3 Legere managed to build up the T-Mobile brand by being the "un-carrier," or basically, by fighting all the policies that annoyed people in their wireless service! What are some problems you can identify in your industry? What actions could you take on social media (granted, you may not be a CEO, but a powerful personal brand leads to a powerful voice) to fight these problems or speak against them? One question I regularly ask myself that helps with this is, "What stirs up my righteous anger?" Your answer will reveal an area where you have strong emotions that something needs to be made right. Is there a cause or idea that comes to mind?

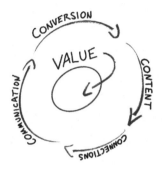

THE 4 CS

I magine, for a moment, that you were a farmer.

Farmers are masters of planning and systematizing their efforts. They know exactly what to plant, and when. You plant corn two to three weeks after the last frost. You plant soybeans in May or June, but certainly no later than June 20th. From there, you follow a very regimented schedule for watering, fertilizer, insecticide treatments, and harvesting. Every farmer knows that there is a proper system & schedule to follow, and if they fail to follow it, then they will not see much from the seeds they planted.

Now, let's say that a farmer planted a tomato seed today and figured they could somehow force it to grow tomatoes within one week. We all know that that's impossible– tomatoes just don't work that way. You could use all the grow lights and fertilizer that you wanted, but it's just not gonna happen. Even worse, imagine planting a seed, never watering it or giving it any sunlight, and then wondering why it won't grow.

Recruiting is the same. You have to create a systemized approach! But often, people get confused here and believe that being a farmer means they can't make it "move faster." So they hang up the farming hat and wear the hunter's hat. Having coached over 1,200 people over the past five years, I can tell you this is false; YOU CAN!!

Building relationships and bringing value will always accelerate the process of recruiting someone. Why? Because your goal shifted from making a transaction with someone to actually caring about them. Your actions support this and relationships form.

> **RECRUITING LEADERS OUT THERE: YOU'RE NOT A HUNTER, YOU'RE A FARMER. HUNTERS ARE CONSTANTLY LOOKING FOR PREY. FARMERS ARE TRYING TO NURTURE GROWTH. THERE'S A HUGE DIFFERENCE.**

It's unfortunate, but the recruiting world often has people thinking they need to be aggressive to move someone along. There is a view of the recruiter as a "hunter." They have to seek out talent aggressively. They have to hunt down recruits. They must be "aggro" if they want to "grow."

I want to put this idea to rest, so I'll repeat it to all the Recruiting Leaders out there: you're not a hunter; you're a farmer. Hunters are constantly looking for prey. Farmers are trying to nurture growth. There's a huge difference.

Do you see growth by getting aggressive with the seed or by nurturing it?

Do you see growth when it's not the season for it? Or do you patiently wait and keep tending to your plants?

Still, even farmers have an almanac to follow for when the right time to plant is. This section will be your guide for the "growing period" of building your brand and recruiting well. Follow this process, and you should start seeing success and growth in their due time.

To make it easier to remember, we've divided this process into 4 Cs . They are as follows:

Content Matters
Connections Matter
Communicating with your Audience Matters
Conversions Matter

So with no further ado, let's jump in and start planting seeds.

Richard Milligan

con·te·nt

content

noun

**What you post– whether it's written, a
picture, or a video.**
I love the content this thought leader puts out.

CONTENT MATTERS

Y ou'll notice, as we go on, that each step influences the other. For instance, more connections will get you more eyeballs on your content. At the same time, more content will help you build more connections. Your content is what will make you more visible to the people you connect with and is the key to how you communicate with your audience. Again, it's a lot like farming. There's a formula for how much sun and water plants need... So the more sun they get, it's often the case that they'll need more water!

Again, I'm going to ask a question that seems simple, but is pretty complicated: Why is visibility important?

Because it's a key component of being an Attractive Leader.

Basically, you want your vision, values, and why to be seen by anyone who might align with them.

Remember Anne? She created content that was seen by a top recruit, and then he messaged her. That's Attractive Leadership at its finest. On social media, you have to be visible to be attractive. Her letters and emails weren't enough—her posts humanized her and moved recruits through the process faster because they knew and trusted her.

People see what you post. The content you post on social media is what could potentially lead to a message down the line from a recruit who is feeling disaffected under their current leader, and recognizes something special in you and your content.

At the same time, this places a lot of pressure on people. I remember when I first started building my personal brand, and I thought I had to be the John Maxwell of recruiting coaching. I had to think of nothing but amazing thought leadership posts like him.

Anybody that's read any of Maxwell's books knows that's a ton of pressure! I remember racking my brain at night to conjure up these awesome thoughts around leadership and recruiting.

But then at some point I realized that not only is that not sustainable, it also leaves out a huge part of who I am, which is the human element. And that's no good because *you* are the most connectable thing in your business.

One thing I want to make clear is that you aren't only a creator of content. You're also a Content Curator.

> **"**
>
> *YOU* ARE THE MOST CONNECTABLE THING IN YOUR BUSINESS.
>
> **"**

A lot of people get into a sales mindset with their content. They feel like they have to make everything about brand, brand, brand, sell, sell, sell. Everything has to be at a professional level, professional video, professional sound, professional graphics, etc. They have to create professional level content for a professional space, right? That means it's about *company* principles and *company* branding.

Except that deprives you of authenticity. Some amount of very high level professional content certainly doesn't hurt.

But that type of content isn't authentic, and it's not sustainable.

It's also worth recalling the main advice I heard from a top recruiter I coached. He'd signed over 85 people in the last year or so, and what he said was that building his personal brand was what made all the difference in attracting so much high level talent.

Remember—your *personal* brand is far more powerful to recruiting than your *company* brand will ever be. So it stands to reason that *personal* content will be a more powerful recruiting tool than *company* content can be.

So how do you build a personal brand? Content curation, rather than content creation.

This is important in part because you need to be posting to social media very very consistently. In an ideal world, that would mean three three to five posts on each platform every day. Since this isn't an ideal world though, and since Recruiting Leaders often have a lot of other duties on their plates, I want you to shoot for at least **one post, per day, on each platform** that you use.

That still sounds like a lot, right? But:

1. You don't have to create all of that content. You just have to curate it.

2. Create your content box. Fill a box with your favorite movies, your favorite books, things that you love. That way when you sit down to write, you just have to write about the first thing your eyes land on.

Pro Tip: Track your ideas using tools like Evernote, or your phone's notes app! You can even create shortcuts that can automatically be added to a Trello board!

3. It doesn't have to be perfect. Very polished and "perfect" content tends to require a lot of time and effort to create. I have a lot of experience, and I'm passionate about my company, but coming up with new content everyday can be a task! And anybody who manages a team or has kids knows, taking the time to put on a suit and film with a camera crew is next to impossible.

This type of content is also not very human, because humans are imperfect. We don't always connect with seeing someone at their most polished and most professional.

A Content Curator understands that the content is there, and that they just need to capture it.

An example: when my kids were young, they were constantly coming up with funny and cute phrases. A short video of them being their silly selves is content that humanizes me and will connect with people. It didn't take any time to "create," because it was already there. The effort of recording a five-year-old is way lower than the effort of renting a studio. And it also demonstrates my biggest why, which is my family.

Now, is this content "perfect?" Of course not. But that's exactly why people will connect with it.

This principle goes beyond videos as well. 4C recently helped a client recognize a great story from his regular everyday life and encouraged him to type it up and post it on his LinkedIn.

He didn't come across perfectly in this story. It was about a time his wife called him out on some less-than-stellar behavior. He wrote a quick post about it, added one of the many random pictures he already had of him and his wife just hanging out, and ended on a note of how grateful he was to have someone in his corner who wasn't afraid to shoot straight with him.

That post went viral within his circle. As of this writing, the post had 96 comments and over 1,000 likes, when this client had about 2,500 connections. People really connected with it.

It didn't feature a professional photo. It didn't mention his business or work at all. It was a story about him failing! And it probably took only a couple of minutes to type up the story and find a good picture in his camera roll.

However, this post demonstrated this client's why, (his family) alongside one of his core values (accountability). And it did that through a funny story about human people. People connect way more with flaws than they ever will with a company logo.

> **PEOPLE CONNECT WAY MORE WITH FLAWS THAN THEY EVER WILL WITH A COMPANY LOGO.**

But how do we craft personal stories into effective posts? An easy exercise is to think of any story that starts with: "I remember." Whatever must have come to mind is something that you remember and that resonates with you. For instance, I might say, "I remember in 2007, which was a tough time for a lot of people..."

HERE'S SOME SPACE TO DO SOME QUICK BRAINSTORMING AROUND "I REMEMBER" STATEMENTS.

WHAT DO YOU REMEMBER?

Richard Milligan

WHAT MEMORIES ARE STICKING OUT TO YOU?

IS THERE ONE IN PARTICULAR THAT FEELS LIKE SOMETHING YOU COULD CRAFT INTO A SHORT POST?

Richard Milligan

EXERCISE: SORT OUT SOME STORY THOUGHTS HERE: I REMEMBER...

I REMEMBER THE FIRST TIME WHEN...

Richard Milligan

I REMEMBER MY FIRST JOB, WHERE...

I REMEMBER THE TIME I FIRST LEARNED THAT...

Richard Milligan

I REMEMBER WHEN I FIRST MET SOMEONE VERY IMPORTANT TO ME...

Now that you have some memories, look toward the present day, and document, document, document. Whatever happens, take note.

For instance: "I got a cool email today..." "We had a team meeting today and something weird happened..." "I had a great conversation today..."

Every day, stories are happening to you and around you. Share them.

Why are stories so important? They connect with our emotions, and people make decisions that go with their gut more easily than their brain. Our emotions will decide something almost within seconds, but our brain will try to debate and logic things out.

EVERY DAY, STORIES ARE HAPPENING TO YOU AND AROUND YOU. SHARE THEM.

You want connections and recruits to be thinking emotionally when they read your content. That's what leads someone to make the decision to make a change—and you could be that change for them.

In content curation, stories are at the heart of the process. If you're living true to the vision, values, and why that drive you, then you'll always be surrounded by stories, pictures, videos, and content that will demonstrate who you are.

Keep in mind that curated content does not always have to be personal either– you can curate content by listening to podcasts, reading books, watching TED talks, or anywhere else you get ideas and inspiration.

One of my all-time favorite books is *Steal Like an Artist* by Austin Kleon, which has some of the most valuable advice: steal like an artist. Don't rob your favorite podcaster, but let them inspire you and build on the ideas you hear. And that's content curation as well. Just as a museum curator selects art pieces and displays them to tell a story, you will find inspiration from many sources to tell your story. With that in mind, here are some more quick exercises.

LIST YOUR 5 FAVORITE MOVIES:

LIST YOUR 5 FAVORITE BOOKS:

Richard Milligan

WHAT IS AN INTERESTING CONCEPT OR IDEA YOU LEARNED ONLINE RECENTLY?

WHAT'S A "FUN FACT" YOU LEARNED FROM SOMEONE RECENTLY?

As you are curating your content, a trick you can use as you are writing it is to make it Evergreen.

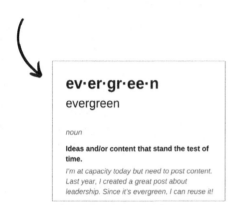

ev·er·gr·ee·n

evergreen

noun

Ideas and/or content that stand the test of time.

I'm at capacity today but need to post content. Last year, I created a great post about leadership. Since it's evergreen, I can reuse it!

Evergreen simply means ideas and content that can be used and reused any day, month, year or season. In other words, this type of content doesn't have to be tied to a specific date like Christmas or Halloween. This type of content is great to have on hand because you can slot it onto social media at any time, and it can be reused to help fill out your posting schedule.

When you're scheduling posts far ahead of time—which will help you stay consistent even when things get busy—then you want this evergreen content to fill out your feed. You don't want to write a post about your birthday only to have it go up months later! Because of this, it's helpful to have a backlog of evergreen posts and ideas to put into your social media scheduler.

It's helpful to review content that you've already created that's tied to a specific time and revise it to be evergreen. Ask yourself—what aspects of this post ties it to that moment in time?

Is it just the tense that you wrote in?

Is it how you've phrased your opening sentence?

It often comes down just changing one or two phrases. For example:

"Last night"

"Last week"

"This weekend"

"My 7-year-old"

To make these posts evergreen, focus instead on using more generic terms like "recently" or leaving out details like ages or dates. So, for example, you could change:

"This past weekend, my 7-year-old daughter, Emma, drew this cartoon"

To

"My daughter Emma once drew this cartoon…"

And remember, the best content pieces to reuse as evergreen content are your memories and stories that you've connected back to your core values.

you start a post with, "When I was ten…" then it becomes evergreen. That memory continues to impact you in the present day.

Once you have a set collection of evergreen content to work with, you can use scheduling tools to help requeuing—scheduling your recycled content in advance—easier. This will help keep your messages consistent, and save you time so you can spend it with the people who matter most to you!

As we exit this C, remember, you are radically human and an Attractive Leader. You just need to communicate that to your audience.

****

POSTING REGULARLY

Whether you use a marketing service or you do it yourself, in order to successfully attract the right people, you have to post to social media regularly. It doesn't have to be your new 9 to 5, but it does need to be a commitment. And in order for it to be a commitment, it has to become a priority. We always protect what is a priority to us.

So, you need to make social media a priority, and you need to make it sustainable. Just posting consistently for 90 days will not change your career. Committing to eating healthy and daily workouts for 90 days, only to stop right after that, won't do much for us in the long run either. Neither will planting a seed and only watering it for a week.

Remember, if the level of commitment is too hard, it's not sustainable. If the workouts are too strenuous, the body will begin to break down. If the food regimen is too limiting, it's just a matter of time before we go back to our old eating habits.

Moral of the story: Find a system that works for you in the long run. This is not a short-term practice. It's a business plan for long-term success.

Several companies I've worked with experience 45-50% no-shows from successful salespeople once a meeting is scheduled. In my coaching, I've directly seen, time and time again, that when a leader is active in social media, it not only reduces the number of no-shows, it reduces it *significantly*.

This makes sense. If I find out that I'm going to have a meeting with you and I look you up and see you're active in social media as a Dynamic Leader, it actually accelerates me. It influences me to be willing to show up at a higher rate because *you* showed up at a higher rate. Your presence on social media also influences whether people accept your offer or someone else's offer. It's certainly a huge piece of the recruiting puzzle!

And this all comes back to our systems. In order to be consistent and efficient, we need to have a system in place. I will next identify some tools and techniques I use to help me with my systems in a digital environment. They should help you to be consistent and, in time, ramp up your content.

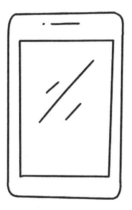

TOOLS & PLATFORMS THAT WILL HELP YOU SUCCEED

A s the Beatles once suggested, we can get by as long as we have a little help from our friends. And in this case, our tools for managing our prospects, our systems, and our calendar are some very, very good friends to have. In this section, I've identified some key tools and techniques that have helped me tremendously in managing my time and my priorities as a recruiter in today's digital world. Keep in mind that social media does change—some of this advice may not be evergreen. Keep an eye on the trends and learn about new tools as they arrive!

First, here's an overview of key tech pieces that I generally recommend for digital recruiting:

KEY TECH PIECES FOR SUCCESS IN A DIGITAL WORLD

Social Platforms: Facebook, LinkedIn, Instagram, Twitter, Tiktok, and Sales Navigator for searching for prospects

Automation Tools: Zapier or Make for automating software between platforms.

Scheduling Tools: Hootsuite, Planable, CoSchedule, Sendable, Buffer, Agorapulse, and Sprout Social

CRMs & Database Software: Pipedrive with LinkMatch, AirTable or Trello

Communication Tools: Email plugins, SlyBroadcast for voicemail, Reach for texting

Systems Trackers: AirTable and Trello

CALENDARS

In order to keep track of your time blocking, the next steps for each prospect on your list, or even keeping track of your social media posts, some sort of calendar tool is essential.

SCHEDULING TOOLS FOR SOCIAL MEDIA

Scheduling tools like Hootsuite, Planable, CoSchedule, Sendable, Buffer, Agorapulse, and Sprout Social will help you schedule your social media posts in advance. This will help save some time as you focus on future content—rather than the daily task of uploading your posts.

For this task, the tools I recommend the most are Plannable and CoSchedule.

Pro tip: CoSchedule even has a feature to help keep "evergreen" content in rotation–as in, posts that can be re-posted months later and still apply to you as a leader and individual, no matter the season. It's okay to reuse content so long as it helps you stay consistent. That's why we recommend writing posts in ways that avoid letting them become "dated" too soon.

CRMS & DATABASE TOOLS

The more we get to know a person, the more information we tend to accumulate. So as we get to know our prospects, we need more and more efficient ways of keeping up with all of the information we receive. CRMS and Database tools like Pipedrive and Airtable are great for managing a lot of information, either with a team or on your own. They are similarly good for helping us plan out posts or store content ideas.

When you have good tools, then your one hour a day (or however long you decide to dedicate to social media each day) can be used at top efficiency. You know your own schedule better than anyone, but with just one hour on Monday, you can plan out and schedule all your posts for the rest of the week.

Then, on Tuesday, you can use that time to research prospects on your social media platforms and record the information you gather.

On Wednesday, you can send messages looking to connect with people.

Thursday could be used to check in with people, or even meet with people once they reach out.

And Friday can be a time to check in, write out some posts, or store content ideas to use when you get back to things on Monday.

This schedule is just one example of many to show how much you can achieve when you block out one hour a day and are willing to embrace the tools available to you.

UNDERSTANDING EACH PLATFORM AND HOW THEY ARE USED

A s I have mentioned, in the digital realm, platforms and their uses are always changing and evolving, so it's essential to keep an eye on trends and changes as they come. The 4C team regularly posts updates about platforms on our online coaching platform—4C University (www.4cu.live).

Below I have outlined the basics of each platform that I use today to establish myself as an Attractive Leader on social media. But before I delve into each platform, a quick note on social media profiles—they are *very* important. No matter what platform you are on, you want to create a good impression with your account profile. It's the first thing people see, and it plays a huge part in a prospect deciding whether or not to connect with you. So on each social media platform you use, make sure you are optimizing your bio, profile photo, and additional information or images associated with your account, depending on the platform's options—highlight covers for Instagram, for instance, are very different from your Linkedin profile pic.

Your profile should tell people WHO you are and WHY they should follow you. You could consider including your job title, your greatest accomplishment, or anything else that's important to you. If you have a link to your website, you should also include that in your profile. How in-depth you want to go in your bio often depends on the platform, but the rule of thumb is to make sure that you have a clear and presentable profile that helps to show your values and who you are as an Attractive Leader.

Similarly, remember that engaging with your audience is key if you want to build a following. In addition to posting on all platforms, we recommend setting a timer and intentionally interacting with other users. This means liking, commenting, following, and even sending DMs when appropriate. The more you engage with someone, the higher your content will appear on their feed (and the more likely they will interact with it). A win-win!

LINKEDIN

LinkedIn is the current leading business-to-business platform, so it should be where you focus the majority of your energy. Specifically, you should work on turning your profile into one that reflects who you are, rather than just a bobblehead for your company.

Many assume that because LinkedIn is a business platform, they can only post business content. That couldn't be any more false. When you switch to utilizing LinkedIn to showcase you as an Attractive Leader, you will see a significant difference in how people respond to your content.

Not only is LinkedIn good for showcasing yourself, but it can also be your number one tool for identifying potential recruits. To provide an example of a written LinkedIn post, I'll use a piece I posted during the pandemic.

I included a photograph I'd taken of the empty shelves from my vantage point where I could see the full shelves at the very top.

This post did very well on LinkedIn– it connected with people. It shared an experience many could connect with, had a visual element, and included a powerful quote from a writer who was much more talented than I could ever be!

LINKEDIN POST

*Fear blinds people!
I went to the grocery store only to find
there weren't many groceries. I happen
to be 6'5" and can see things and places
that most can't. I proceeded to buy the
regular items which happened to be out
of sight/reach for most people.
As I walked around the store, I caught
people staring at me. It took me a while
to figure it all out. I had a full basket in a
store where it appeared there weren't
many groceries to be had.
Then it hit me.
In uncertain times people operate out
of fear and in doing so they miss opportunities all around them.
Fear blinds people.
Fear paralyzes.
Fear clouds decision-making abilities.
Faith opens eyes to things before unseen.
I love this quote from an old book by C.S. Lewis.
"If we are all going to be destroyed by an atomic bomb, let that bomb when it
comes find us doing sensible and human things — praying, working, teaching,
reading, listening to music, bathing the children, playing tennis, chatting to our
friends over a pint and a game of darts — not huddled together like frightened
sheep and thinking about bombs. They may break our bodies, but they need not
dominate our minds."
Live out of faith! In doing so, you will see opportunities everywhere.
#richardnugget
#4crecruiting
#leadstrong*

FACEBOOK

An oldie but still a goodie! From using Facebook to document your daily life to researching potential recruits for more insight into their interests, Facebook is an excellent resource for establishing your personal brand and prospecting.

Although its support among the younger generations is dwindling compared to the newer platforms, Facebook is still effective in reaching the 35 to 65-year-old age group. There are many different ways you can connect with your audience on Facebook, including Facebook Groups and Stories.

Now, how would that LinkedIn post from before need to be changed for Facebook? In terms of the writing and photograph, it could be broadly the same as the LinkedIn post example above. However, I would not include hashtags. Hashtags increase engagement on LinkedIn and other platforms, but they don't do much for you on Facebook.

TWITTER

Twitter differentiates itself from other social media because it is a micro-blogging platform. It is best used to receive breaking news, follow trending topics, and get out important messages quickly and concisely.

Currently, it is estimated that a little less than half of the U.S. population uses the app daily, with the majority of users being male. One of the best ways you can use Twitter to build up your brand is by engaging in important conversations surrounding topics that matter to your industry the most.

In terms of written content (using the examples from above), Twitter features very short blurbs. In this case, I would have to edit my thoughts even more!

I would probably go ahead and include the picture as well, but it's not as much of a requirement. Twitter is a microblogging platform, so words tend to get you pretty far.

TWITTER POST

Got weird looks at the grocery store. Why? My basket was full, but the store looked empty. I'm tall and saw all the items on the top shelves.

We're all afraid right now. Fear blinds people, but faith opens eyes to things before unseen.

#richardnugget #4crecruiting #leadstrong

INSTAGRAM

Instagram is a photo sharing platform that, much like Facebook, is helpful for documenting your daily life and researching potential recruits for more insight into their interests. While Instagram is generally thought of as a place to connect with friends and family, it has become increasingly popular to connect with influencers, businesses, and even potential employers. The app has numerous features and post styles, and the best practice is to utilize all of these features. In recent years, Instagram has undergone numerous changes to remain competitive with emerging social media platforms. Since the app is known to make frequent changes, it is important to stay informed about the current practices that are best.

Since Instagram is a very visual platform, I would greatly shorten the written post (also provided in LinkedIn and Instagram above) and take some more pictures of the store, the shelves, and my basket.

In this case, the caption to these pictures could be something like:

INSTAGRAM POST

I was getting weird looks at the grocery store the other day. Why? Because my basket was full, but the store looked empty. I'm a tall guy, and could see all the items on the top shelves that nobody else was noticing.

We're all operating from a lot of stress and fear right now, and it's blinded us to the opportunities that exist if we choose to look just a little more.

Fear blinds people. Fear paralyzes. Fear clouds decision-making abilities. Faith opens eyes to things before unseen.

#richardnugget
#4crecruiting
#leadstrong

TIKTOK

TikTok, the newest of the social media platforms, is focused on short-form videos. While TikTok is mainly thought of as being a platform just for Gen Z, the fastest growing demographic on the site is 30+-year-olds.

TikTok is a great place to establish your personal brand as its algorithm focuses on providing viewers with niche content that aligns with them.

Where TikTok differs from other platforms is that, rather than just documenting your daily life, TikTok will push your content more if you focus on a niche. Your niche <u>does not</u> have to be anything industry or job-related. If you're super into grilling or have a fun hobby, you can find more algorithmic gains by focusing your content on what you are passionate about. Look at your personas and ask yourself if there's one that you think would lead to some great short video content.

To continue with the content example I've used for the other platforms, my best bet would probably be to take a short video where I start at the bottom, pan my camera up the "empty" shelves, until we see the full shelves at the top. Then I could say something like, "When you're worried there's nothing, keep looking!"

Pro Tip: As you see in the various examples above, repurpose your content. For example, it's easy to take a post you made for Facebook and repurpose it on LinkedIn. Or take a story you shared on LinkedIn and create a leadership video that you could post on any of your social media platforms.

CASE STUDY:
NATALIE OVERTURF

N atalie Overturf is a veteran of the mortgage industry, with over 30 years of experience. In that time, she's been a top originator and has built a career as a respected leader. She's also an avid runner, the co-founder of a med spa, and the proud mother of twin girls.

And in the last year, she hired more than 40 of the top people to the sales division of her team. Those numbers don't show up out of anywhere—she's dedicated time and effort to building a strong social media presence, and she's seeing the rewards of doubling down on attractive leadership.

"I have had many recruits tell me that they get a picture of how I lead and what it would be like to work for me from my social media posts. Social media gives them a glimpse into who I am, my values, what's important to me and my personality. It reduces the time the candidate needs to spend getting to know me."

This wasn't easy for her. Like many people, she wasn't always comfortable with sharing her emotions over social media. She understood the value of this—both on a personal level and a professional level—and doubled down on creating an open and vulnerable presence.

Neuroscientist Antonio Damasio famously said: "We are not thinking machines that feel; rather, we are feeling machines that think."

In his book, *Self Comes to Mind,* Damasio proposed the idea that memories are encoded through emotions. Basically, when an experience causes a big emotional reaction, we remember it better. Whether it's happiness, sadness, or any other emotion, that feeling will make the memory stick out much more than our regular day-to-day experiences.

This applies to social media as well. Content that isn't afraid to be emotional tends to stick out more and stick with us better. We remember the content that engages with us emotionally precisely because it makes us feel something new.

Think of it like this—how many internet ads have you seen? How many do you remember?

Now, can you recall a piece of content that made you feel something? I'm sure we can all think of at least one video of a soldier reuniting with their dog or at least one LinkedIn post in which the writer shared a story about a relative who had since passed away. We can all recall the content that has made us cry—whether it's happy or sad tears!

Natalie is incredible at her business, but she's also doubled down on content that people will remember. Later, when a potential recruit is feeling unhappy at work and wondering what else is out there, they'll be able to remember a post that Natalie shared about her passion for leadership. They'll remember that post precisely because it stood out and made them feel a real emotional connection with her.

"I have had recruits comment on my posts, and that has allowed me to message them and invite them into a deeper conversation. Social media makes your interaction more personal. You are no longer one dimensional."

Natalie has built a presence that gives people on the outside a view of the inside– they see a leader who is dedicated to her team and is willing to communicate with them. They get an idea of what it would be like to work for her, and they like how it looks!

Most of all, you should absorb this insight that Natalie had to share:

"You are a person with thoughts, feelings, opinions, etc. That's the most important part of attracting the right people to your team."

Richard Milligan

co·nn·ec·tion
connection

noun

The people who friend and follow you on social media.
Thnaks for accepting my friend request! I'm looking forward to seeing your posts and updates!

CONNECTIONS MATTER

I f you want to connect with someone online for business, where do you start?

Most people will say LinkedIn because it is a business networking platform. But all platforms can—and should—be used for building relationships. Most of this section will cover LinkedIn, however, keep in mind that these key principles apply to most social media networks in 2022. For example, Facebook can be a very valuable tool for letting the "human" side of yourself shine alongside the "professional" side.

Why does building connections matter? In some ways, this seems obvious, but it's always important to me to establish the why behind any of the advice I'm giving you.

So... why does building connections matter?

WHY DOES BUILDING CONNECTIONS MATTER?

1. If I connect with someone now, I have access to their inbox. And often, that inbox is tied to their email. If I send them a message on LinkedIn, for instance, they will get a message in their email inbox alerting them of that message. That's a powerful level of access.

2. Connections build what we call "Social Proof."

What is "Social Proof?" It's a term that Robert Cialdini coined back in 1984 in his book *Influence*. This phenomenon is also called informational social influence, and essentially it's the idea that people copy the actions of others in an attempt to emulate behavior in certain situations– the larger the group that is behaving a certain way, the more "social proof" there is. So, for instance:

"Eighty-three percent of consumers recommend a brand they follow on social to friends and family."

"Ninety-one percent of shoppers read online reviews before making a purchase."

"Eight two percent of Americans ask for referrals and recommendations from family and friends before making any kind of purchase."

People seek out the opinions of others, and they trust others to show them what is "good." So the more people who like your content, the more others will also perceive it as being good.

Essentially, there is a perception of influence that increases with the number of connections someone has. I have over 50,000 followers on LinkedIn. People see that, and they are given Social Proof that I'm worth following. The more followers you have, the more proof you have that your influence and content matter. Back in the day, we established trust with someone with a firm handshake. Nowadays, it's all about how many people can be seen engaging with your Social Media.

3. Engagement increases when you have followers, and engagement provides another level of social proof. LinkedIn says that only 10-15% of your connections will even *see* any post that you put out. And of those who see it, you can never be sure how many will engage with it. Only about 1% of LinkedIn 260 million monthly users were shown to share posts regularly, for instance. According to Hootsuite: "Most social media marketing experts agree that a good engagement rate is between 1% to 5%."

It's a numbers game. You want more connections so that you can get more eyeballs on your content, and the more potential engagement, which will provide more social proof. A post with 280 likes and 65 comments gets more reach, and is, therefore, more likely to be seen by the people you want to attract.

The long and short of it is that people are more willing to connect with someone who has a higher level of social proof. From there, people are much more willing to have that first conversation with you.

Essentially, more connections equal more engagement. More engagement equals more social proof. More social proof equals more Attractive Recruiting.

Connections matter. That means building processes to help you build connections, not just with potential recruits, but with anyone within your industry who will connect with what you do.

Of course, part of that will rely on the content you're producing on social media.

PROSPECTING:
IDENTIFY YOUR AVATAR

W hen creating a list of prospects that you want to connect with, you want to identify the ideal person you want to recruit. That will help you identify who in your market is your ideal "avatar".

"Avatar" refers to your ideal candidate profile. For instance, maybe I'm not particularly interested in entry-level candidates or people who would have to move a great distance. In this case, my ideal candidate has at least seven years of experience in the industry and lives within a certain radius of my business. I want a list of people like that.

av·at·ar

avatar

noun

The model match for your team that you use to create your prospect list.

That means identifying: What's a model match for my team? Then, conducting research based on this model.

And the list you create is what allows you to move towards making first contact.

The steps look like this:

1. Make the list.
2. Identify the people in your market.
3. Where are they on Facebook? What's their LinkedIn profile? Where are they on other social platforms like Instagram or Twitter? What are their cell numbers? Their email addresses? If I can get local addresses, that's even better.

Pro tip: Once you identify that avatar, there are a number of platforms and tools you can use in any industry to help build out your list. The tools I recommend for identifying prospects is LinkedIn's Sales Navigator. It has a ton of search filters to identify people around their location and job history. In the mortgage and real estate industries there is MobilityRE also known as MMI. It connects you with the mortgage and real estate production numbers of those within your search criteria. Whatever your industry may be, there may be a similar tool available to you.

Then, when you have built out your list, it's time to make the first contact. You have to do this quickly and through sustained, consistent effort. Jim Collins talks about this concept in his book *Good to Great*. He identifies it as "The Flywheel Effect":

"No matter how dramatic the end result, good-to-great transformations never happen in one fell swoop. In building a great company or social sector enterprise, there is no single defining action, no grand program, no one killer innovation, no solitary lucky break, no miracle moment. Rather, the process resembles relentlessly pushing a giant, heavy flywheel, turn upon turn, building momentum until a point of breakthrough, and beyond." — Jim Collins.

And that's a very good way of describing this process. Once you've made your list, you've started the flywheel.

A flywheel stores kinetic energy over the time dedicated to it being turned, but it takes an enormous amount of effort to keep the flywheel moving. You'll have to be willing to put in that effort for the first, second, fifth, tenth, fiftieth, and even one hundredth time. At some point, however, as the flywheel stores kinetic energy, it eventually turns effortlessly on its own.

It's not going to turn effortlessly right now. It's going to take an enormous amount of energy to get this thing started. So at the outset, you've got to put some muscle into it.

To do that, from the list phase, you identify the people in your market who you want to actually make contact with—those who don't just fit your search criteria, but that also align with who you want on your team. Researching your prospects not only helps you generate a lit, but it also helps you find ways to affirm them in messages.

Pro Tip: The way to stand out in messages is by tailoring them to each individual. This goes beyond just adding their name to a copy/pasted message, it's adding in affirmation that you actually LOOKED at their profile and are actively interested in THEM.

Once you have reached out, you have established the relationship bridge, which is what we do as recruiters. We build relationships. And we first need to build a bridge to get us there.

Once that relationship bridge is built, you can show up every single month with something of a real tangible value to offer your prospect. Look for something that will help them grow their business or will help them solve problems in some way.

Every weak leader in your market should be nervous about this. Their people are going to get an enormous amount of value from you every single month, forever. All through your very simple plan:

1. Identify talent
2. Make first contact (establish the relationship bridge)
3. And then bring them value again, again, and again

It's certainly not rocket science. But it does require some initial muscle and sustained, consistent effort on your part to keep the connection (and the "flywheel") alive.

co·mm·un·ic·at·ing

communicating with your audience

noun

Directly reaching out to specific people on a one-on-one level over social media.

I've been in communication with a top recruit who also happens to be a very cool person.

COMMUNICATING WITH YOUR AUDIENCE MATTERS

T his third C ties into the others we've already discussed. In some way your content is already one form of communicating with your audience But you need to go a step further. Always message your audienc When someone– but particularly a potential recruit– accepts a connectic request, send them a message. The only trouble is that most people don understand what types of messages to send.

A lot of people think it should be a "right hook".

I'm here to tell you—don't ever send a right hook, right out of the gate.

You don't show up on LinkedIn and say, "Oh, by the way, I'm hiring. Oh, t the way, here's the 10 bullet points that you should look at that represent wh my company is amazing. Can we meet?"

No. That's a right hook nobody wants to be hit by. And it's not an effectiv system.

Recruiting is about relationship-building. Patience is where great recruiter win.

Instead try this quick script on LinkedIn. (though try to bring your ow personal brand and flavor to your messages!).

"Hi (new connection)! Thanks for connecting with me– I've endorsed your to skills, and I love your post about _____. I look forward to engaging wit you here on LinkedIn!"

You'll notice that at this point, you've already brought them value t endorsing them. Any time you message, try to bring value however you ca whether it's through a useful article, podcast, or video that you saw. Thes messages can take a form as simple as this:

"Hi (insert their name), I read this great TedTalk that I think you'll also like. hope it brings some value to your day."

One thing you will also notice, is that nowhere in the messages does it __as__ for anything in return. They do not ask for purchases, phone calls, recruitir messages, etc. When you're giving value, it has to be something that is valuab to your audience and gives no benefit back to you. There is a time and a plac for recruiting conversations, and initial messages are not it. I will cove messages that contain an ask in the section on conversions, but I advise you n to skip ahead as it will be detrimental to your recruiting efforts.

Communication also means listening and reacting. Engage with you newsfeed. When a connection makes a post that resonates with you– like it! Leave a comment! This doesn't take much time– a comment can be as short as:

"Great post [their name]! Thanks for sharing some wisdom today!"

This will go miles toward helping them feel a greater connection with you, and it will bring value to them by elevating their content. At the same time, if someone comments on your post, *comment back.* It looks pretty arrogant to see someone take the time to read and respond to your ideas, and then to give them the cold shoulder! Even something as simple as this is plenty:

"Thanks! It's great to know this resonated with you."

Social Media often relies on the law of reciprocity. When you're commenting on someone's posts, they want to comment on yours. Then your content reads as better to the algorithm, and you are able to build more social proof. It's a really great feedback loop.

Often, I'll also communicate with my audience by sending a message to people who even just *liked* my content. I'll say something as simple as:

"Thanks for engaging with my content. It means a lot to me."

I've provided these scripts just to give an idea of how fast and easy communication can be, but I want you to try to draft a few right now, and try to put your voice and personal brand into these scripts. If you have a specific recruit in mind right now, perhaps tailor your scripts toward that person. Remember– they don't have to be long to provide a lot of value, but the key thing is DO. NOT. SELL. and DO. NOT. RECRUIT.

MINI EXERCISE:
QUICK SCRIPTS

On the following pages, create your own scripts. These can be notes that you refine later, or completed ones.

SCRIPT 1: A MESSAGE TO A NEW CONNECTION.

SCRIPT 2: A MESSAGE SHARING SOMETHING OF VALUE

SCRIPT 3: A COMMENT ON AN AWESOME POST

Richard Milligan

SCRIPT 4: A RESPONSE TO A COMMENT OR LIKE ON YOUR POST

More than anything, remember that you have to be consistent with this communication. Set aside some time every day—even just half an hour—to send some messages, share some value, and communicate. When you do this, you aren't just talking, you're demonstrating your vision, values, and why through the actions you take.

And those are what will turn Communication into Conversions.

Richard Milligan

> **MEASURE YOUR TREASURE OR YOUR TROUBLE WILL DEFINE YOU**

A BRIEF WORD OF CAUTION:
BE AWARE OF THE FAV STAGE

E very leader has what we've termed the "FAV" stage when it comes to building their brand on social media.

FAV stands for:

FEARFUL – People are afraid of being too true and vulnerable on social media. They want to keep things private or avoid sharing too much of themselves or their home life.

AMBIGUOUS – People prefer to be vague rather than be polarizing. They're focused on the potential negative effect of being polarizing, which is that it can push some people away. They end up pleasing everyone while attracting no one.

VACILLATING – People very often have a stage where they go back and forth, feeling like: "I'm no good. I'm awesome. I suck. Everybody loves me. I'm the worst." It's easy to feel this way on social media, where every "like" gives us a dopamine hit, and every negative comment (or even worse– no reaction at all) does the opposite.

The cure for FEAR is vulnerability. You don't have to share things like your home address. And don't share any family details that everybody isn't comfortable with; but sharing your failures and hard truths will often result in connections that will surprise you. And recruits will feel even better because they know they're connecting with the real and complete you. Don't ever let fear guide you or change you.

The cure for AMBIGUITY is confidence. Your vision, values, and why all matter. Refer back to your "Why I do this" statements if you ever need a reminder of how important these are to you. They're definitely too important to be watered down for someone who was never going to get it anyway, and being polarizing has a powerful ability to attract the right people as much as it will push away the wrong people.

The cure for VACILLATING is objectivity. We all feel our feelings sometimes, and that's fine, but take a moment to be objective about things. Are you really the worst, or did you just see one moment of failure that you can learn from? Are you really the best, or did you have a post that did well and can provide another learning opportunity? For some leaders, it might be best to turn off any alerts from social media and instead dedicate a certain time of day to looking over your new likes and comments. That way your mood isn't subject to each new "ding" of your phone.

I'm sharing this FAV framework because everybody goes through this. And that's okay. Think of this disclaimer as being similar to when you go to the doctor and they say, "This shot might hurt for a day or so, but then it will be over and you'll be healthier."

Better yet, as long as we're thinking like farmers, consider this, there is always a stage, with any plant, where you're waiting for it to take root. That stage can look pretty dicey from the outside because everything is happening underground, where you can't see much progress. At that point, it's easy to get in your head and wonder if anything you're doing is helping at all. Are the water and sun helping? Is the fertilizer doing anything?

But once you see the sprouts, you'll know that there's been progress.

I'm warning everyone reading this that there will be a "growing pains" stage while you build up your brand! There will be a stage where you're constantly second-guessing yourself and wondering if you should change how you present yourself. There will even be a stage where you wonder if anything you're doing is making a difference at all.

But all that's happening is that your brand and content are taking root. And in time, you'll start to see the fruits of your labor.

Sit with those feelings, sure, but also recognize them as normal. These are standard aches and pains. When we're feeling bad, it's easy to assume that that means something's going wrong, but this is all just a regular part of the process. It might hurt for a minute, but you and your leadership will be healthier for having done this!

Above all—avoid letting this FAV stage affect how you post. Would a farmer dig up a seed just because they can't tell if it's taken root yet? Of course not. They would keep watering it and nurturing it as always.

You should always post content that's consistently true to you, rather than uprooting yourself to please someone else. And focus on the good. Something I'm known for saying is, "Measure your treasure or your trouble will define you." Even when there's bad news in the industry or economy, share something you've learned or that helps you during challenging times. Once again, the goal is to add value—not more noise.

CASE STUDY:
EDDY PEREZ

I f anyone's familiar with the highs and lows of being an Attractive Leader on social media, it's Eddy Perez.

As co-founder and CEO of Equity Prime Mortgage (EPM), he's gone viral more than once since he first doubled down on social media back in 2015. Often, this was a positive thing: Eddy is the child of Cuban immigrants. He's had posts go viral by sharing his father's story of coming to America in a rowboat, or just a simple story about how happy he was that his mother had the energy to visit him at work after battling cancer two times.

After a friend and coworker first told him that he needed to get on Social, Eddy admits he was skeptical. "I was 38 at the time. It was just one of those things like, I don't know if this will really work out or really matter."

However, he trusted this friend's advice, and continued to post. Consistency, in his opinion, is key to leadership and to social media. "The trick is that you gotta stay consistent because you never know which post or which message is gonna resonate the most. And a lot of times it's really about a consistent message."

He saw this in action himself, when a post about his father went viral. Eddy is the child of Cuban immigrants, and his father escaped oppression by coming to America in a rowboat.

"I remember it was 2017 on my father's birthday. I wrote that piece, that at that time made it to 25,000 or something impressions. And then a lot of people started walking up to me at a mortgage conference talking about it, and I said, holy crap. This has a bigger landscape than I thought. People within the organization who read that and didn't know some of my father's journey and how I felt about him said that that helped give them better insight into me as a leader.

Since then, Eddy's seen his share of the bright side of Attractive Leadership He's had many more posts go viral, and has doubled down at EPM by making a concerted effort to get the other people there to become active on social media and it's paying off.

"We have a very good engagement on social throughout our organization And it's growing. It did have to start with me showing the way the most fo years. I mean, I'd say it's only been in the last year or two that it's really hone itself where people are doing videos, they're being vulnerable."

Leaders, CEOs, or anyone else– take note here. You have to lead the charge

Eddy jokes about how often people tell him that they like his conten because he's so "real" on social media. "I don't know what is considered rea Like, I don't know what content is more 'real.'" After all, he's just posting abou his life, his work, or whatever sports news has caught his interest that day.

So what *does* it mean to be "real" on social media? Eddy Perez might not know the exact answer (some people are naturals at being natural) but authenticity is key to Attractive Leadership, and it's often one of the most difficult steps for recruiters to achieve. So what can we learn from Eddy's example?

1. His content isn't particularly geared towards recruiting.

"I don't care if somebody comes and works here or not. And what I mean is, sure. Would I wanna get more people? Of course, we're always recruiting. Of course, we want great people." But his goal in what he posts is entirely around whether the content "impacted somebody else, gave somebody clarity, or even helped the leader before they made other moves."

"Real" content doesn't need to have a sales pitch. It just needs to represent who you are.

2. He creates content that's true to his value systems. "People don't understand that culture is the mentality of the organization. It's how you live and demonstrate your virtues and beliefs. You can have your beliefs, but you also have to have the behaviors that drive it." A good example is Perez often posts about making opportunities for other Hispanic people in the mortgage industry. At the same time, he served a great deal of time on the board of NAHREP (National Association of Hispanic Real Estate Professionals) where he took direct action to do just that. Basically, his posts feel "real" because he's walking the walk *while* he talks the talk. "I don't think companies should have mission statements anymore. Instead, our mission should be to live out our values. And equally important, teach others how to live them as well. Because a lot of people ask, 'How do you live that belief?' Well, here are the behaviors...the purest definition of core values is your behavior, your actions."

3. He's not afraid to be vulnerable.

"Being vulnerable is actually a good thing, you know. It's what makes social media so powerful. People want to see the scars. They don't want the perfect commercials we saw as kids.

Instead, now people want to know: You've got some resilience; you know how to overcome adversity. And you're willing to talk about difficult subjects."

Creating "real" content means opening yourself up and showing who you really are. No one is perfect or unscarred. We all have difficulties and failures in our lives, and people connect with that. We've already said in this book that you are your company's most valuable product. Because of that, it might be easy to think that you have to present a perfect flawless product like we see on commercials. But as Eddy points out– your value comes, in part, from what you've overcome, failures and all. That's where you find real content that can provide real value.

Vulnerability isn't easy, but as Perez puts it, "If you really wanna be a true leader that lifts people up for their best interest, regardless how uncomfortable you make them, you've gotta be more uncomfortable than they could ever be."

Attractive Leadership very much comes down to being "real." People are drawn to authenticity and genuine expression. Nobody remembers the average ad copy from a company website, but people come up to Eddy Perez at events to mention a post he made over five years ago.

"It's recruited what I call our cultural employees. So Mortgage Brokers, Real Estate Agents and Builders have seen commentary. They kind of know who your brand is...and they're your biggest fans."

This is Attractive Leadership at its finest. And it's probably what makes his content feel so "real." There's no sales pitch. It's just about providing value to others.

At the same time, while Perez has reaped the benefits of Attractive Leadership in many ways, he's also seen what many might call the nightmare scenario when they're a public facing leader.

In what was a true PR nightmare, EPM was featured in a very negative– and very one-sided– story on Fox News in 2020. Until EPM could get their side of the story out there, the company, and Eddy specifically, saw a flood of hate over social media. At one point, it escalated into a bomb threat being called into their headquarters, forcing employees to evacuate.

Again, this is what we could very comfortably call the "nightmare scenario" when we enter the public eye. We see many people hesitant to be too available or open over social media in part because the backlash is often so harsh.

What did Eddy Perez do?

"I stayed true. I wasn't gonna listen to people who didn't have their facts straight. They didn't know what they were talking about... it's really easy to send messages online and be an electronic tough guy, you know?"

In a way, he says, he was honored. For a few days EPM was listed as one of the top 10 companies to hate in America, alongside much heavier hitters like Disney and Nike.

Most fear comes down to a fear of the "unknown." It's like when a little kid is afraid of the dark, but they stop being afraid when you turn on the light—the child can see what's in the room now. When we're afraid of the worst case scenario, it's usually because we don't know what will happen. In this case, it might be helpful to look at what Eddy and EPM did and gain some certainty around what to do when the worst happens.

His main advice when this kind of thing happens would be: "You must have a good PR team. I called my CEO peer group and they found us someone who handles situations like that extremely well."

They advised him not to post over the weekend, as this had happened on a Thursday. But he was back to posting by the next week. "I put a very clear message on Twitter and I stuck with it. I leveraged social media and after that, people were going to say whatever they were going to say."

After that, this kind of incident is just a waiting game. Eddy knew that the social media news cycle moves fast, and he knew that the real truth would come out under the careful guidance of his team (and a defamation lawsuit). From there, the people who mattered would know what had really happened. Anybody who wanted to keep holding a grudge was probably too much of an extremist to get it in the first place. "That's the other thing I know: 'In today—gone tomorrow.'"

So at the end of the day, the worst case scenario wasn't quite as devastating as it might seem to us on the outside. At the very least, it's survivable.

And according to Perez, the value gained from being so active on social media is worth the pain. "I get more out of the people who come up to me and say stuff like, 'Man, this really impacted me. I was having a rough day. Or I was picking between two employers and I thought about certain things I'd read, and it helped me ask a few questions. I got the clarity I needed, and now I'm at a job that I love."

Richard Milligan

BECOMING AN
ATTRACTIVE LEADER

H ave you ever thought about what is the most connectable part of you? Before you answer, perhaps it is best to define "connectable." The root word of connectable is "connect." In Latin, it means "a binding or joining together."

So connect-able would mean you are able to join/bind together.

Let's add the word recruit into the mix. It comes from a word in old French, "recrue," which means "new growth." So, to recruit means to add new growth.

With that insight, I don't really see recruiting and connecting as being separate. If you are going to create new growth, you need to be able to join/bind together. So to become a successful recruiter, you must be a connectable recruiter.

For example, let's return to our farmer metaphor for a moment. If you're a farmer, and want new growth in your crop, you can't simply rely on the seed to produce on its own. The seed needs to be able to put down roots, which join and bind it with the earth. You need to foster that connection with water, and adequate sunlight. Growth does not happen in isolation. It requires connections of multiple elements to work together in order to bear fruit. And as a recruiter, your soil, water, and sunlight really boils down to your humanity (which, let's be honest, is quite refreshing in an increasingly digital world).

If your goal is to become a connectable recruiter, you better be ready to be really, really human. That is the most connectable part of you. Most Recruiting Leaders are trying to use digital to circumvent the need to be connectable. Many have bought into the lie that because there are tens of thousands of people that you now have access to, you can reduce your recruiting to a numbers game. I am not sure I can shout in the form of writing in a book, but here is my best attempt at this...

Richard Milligan

STOP TRYING TO SHORTCUT CREATING MEANINGFUL CONNECTIONS!

To fully understand social media, you must realize that the most connectable part of it is that it's made up of a bunch of humans. Humans are ridiculously interesting! Here are a few reasons why:

We have massive failures.
We have beautiful moments.
We have funny situations.
We have incredulous situations.
We grow families.
We build businesses.
We build teams.
We lose opportunities.
We have mutual relationships.
We travel the world.
We catch epic sunsets.
We crash on gnarly ocean waves.
We sing amazing songs.
We celebrate our highlights.
We grieve losses.

I could write pages of examples around moments that are connectable.

By contrast, meet the average Recruiting Leader on social media. Here is what would be typical for what they post around:

We are hiring.
Come join the winning team.
Leadership quote by another thought leader.
A corporate video around a new product.
Generic posts celebrating holidays.

Over the past decade, just a handful of leaders have embraced the idea that social media allows us to accelerate humanizing ourselves to our recruiting audience.

Think about this—if you have a social media presence and you are set to full public, then a lot of information is available. At any moment, someone can plug into your accounts and fully know you. *If* you have humanized yourself.

I can't tell you how many times over the past 5 years someone messaged me on one of my social platforms and said something along the lines of: "I read all of your articles, watched hours of your YouTube videos, scrolled through your LinkedIn posts and I am reaching out because I know I want to hire you as my coach."

It is typical that most Monday mornings I come into my office with multiple people messaging me asking how to sign up for my coaching. It's become so normal that I would be surprised if it didn't happen.

We are our most connectable when we share the truest version of ourselves. **People choose their leader because of what they represent.** People will not know what you represent if you don't show it. This means showing your core values, what direction are you going (vision), and what drives you to go beyond collecting a paycheck (why).

People *want* to be a part of that greater purpose. It's part of the framework of Attractive Leadership and a key component of social proof discussed earlier. As we open ourselves up, people are more drawn to us, creating a positive ripple effect.

Here's an example of what I mean. In 1996, a classic movie came out titled *Jerry Maguire*. It won five Oscar nominations and three Golden Globe nominations and made over a quarter of a billion dollars at the box office.

In the film, a sports agent embarks on a long journey to start his own business geared around a 25-page mission statement called "The Things We Think and Do Not Say." In it, he decried the dishonesty Maguire felt existed within the sport business. He had realized that his dream was to find athletes who would align with his value system and buy into the larger vision—he wanted to do business in a way true to his vision, values, and why. He felt that more was available in the agent and athlete relationship. The movie culminates in Rod, the key athlete in the movie, getting a large contract only made available through overcoming struggles and unifying with his agent.

There are two fantastic moments towards the end.

One is where Rod is being interviewed on TV and the announcer breaks the news of his large contract. Rod gives about a minute of shout outs to his family and to the sports franchise. Then, he pauses and tearfully says, "Wait, wait, wait, I am forgetting somebody. Jerry Maguire, my agent. You are my ambassador of Quan."

The other moment takes place in an earlier scene, where these two had a moment with all of the cameras around them post-game. They embrace and Rod says, "We did it." A competing agent and their athlete watch this moment unfold, and the athlete asks his agent, "Why don't we have that relationship?"

That was just one person who saw what Jerry was doing and realized that they wanted something similar. Can you imagine how these moments, shared in today's digital world, would have accelerated the growth of Jerry's business? He was an Attractive Leader with a high core value system, clarity around the vision for what he was building and his greater purpose for why he was doing it. Given a larger social platform (like social media), he would be unstoppable.

This wasn't a fairytale story. It had conflict and struggle all over it. And that human element was what made the story so effective.

Again, *Jerry Maguire* was a wildly popular and successful movie. People connected to a fictional character who had doubled down on being true to his values. If this story happening in fiction connects with so many people, imagine how seeing similar things play out in reality could connect.

Over the years, I have found that most leaders' stories better align with Jerry Maguire's story over the one they are telling in social media.

When we humanize ourselves on social media:

1. It allows someone to see if their values are aligned with ours.
2. It allows someone to see if we have real value to bring to them.
3. It accelerates trust building.
4. It creates aha's around what you have in common.
5. It creates aha's around who you have in common.

When it comes to creating their personal brand, leaders have one huge problem. There is a major disconnect between humanizing themselves and thinking they need to sell themselves. Having had the chance to work with leaders closely around this, I found there are three types of leaders in social media. They are...

1. The leader who doesn't have or manage their digital brand. They have been successful in the past without having one and believe digital is a waste of time. Let's coin this leader as the *"It's a waste of time"* leader.

2. The leader who thinks they are doing it right in digital, but they post generic company template content. They have generic profile pages in social media with limited connections, generic content, no engagement, and no plan for making a conversion. Let's coin this leader as the *"It's necessary but not essential"* leader.

3. The leader who is actually doing it right. This leader is connectable from the first look at their profile page in social media. They are growing their connections, have personalized content, have great engagement, and have an intentional plan for making a conversion. Let's coin this leader as the *"It's essential to accelerate team growth"* leader.

Let's take a look at these three types and what can be learned from each.

Leader 1: It's a waste of time

Most leaders try social but don't sustain social. Isn't this true of most things in this world? In late 2018, I determined that part of my digital brand would be

a podcast. Today, I am 78 episodes in on my podcast, *Recruiting Conversation*
Before I started the podcast, I researched how many Recruiting Lead
podcasts there were. I was excited that it amounted to ZERO. When I search
the words "Recruiter" and "Recruiting," I found a lot of podcasts that made it
single digit episodes and then disappeared.

In 2021, the data showed that 90% of podcasts don't get past episode 3.
the remaining podcasts, another 90% quit after 20 episodes. To be in the t
1% most productive podcasts in the world, you only need to publish
episodes.

If you are going to get good at anything, you must stick with it AND you mu
understand it. Because the platforms are constantly changing, you have tw
options. One: hire it out as you aren't able or willing to commit the time
learning it. Two: learn it and build your own system for growing yo
connections, creating content, communicating with your audience, a
converting opportunities.

Leader 2: It's necessary but not essential

Some see social media as necessary since people may search them onlir
You can identify these people right away when you search for them. They ha
generic profiles with dated pictures. Beyond that, there is very lit
information about them. At best, this leader is neutral in being able to be se
as an Attractive Leader. It's hard to move towards this if you are a recru
looking for your next opportunity.

At worst, they can appear as not being all in, as being non-relevant, and
lacking understanding of social media.

Leader 3: It's essential

This leader considers digital personal branding a priority. When you tru
have a priority, you protect that priority. You make time where other leade
say time doesn't exist.

A recent study showed that the average professional spends 28% of t
workday reading and responding to email. It seems we believe email is
priority. The reason must be that we have connected internal communicati
as critical to success. But, the leader who believes personal branding
important recognizes that external communication is critical to success.

Connectable recruiting is showing people on the Outside what it is like to
on the Inside, while still on the Outside. One can accomplish this
externalizing what is typically only seen by team members. When they do th
they are using a cheat code to attract top talent in our increasingly digital wor

LEADERSHIP IN THE
NEW DIGITAL AGE

I remember a conversation I had with an executive leader once. In it they articulated their belief that recruiting isn't any more than understanding that people only want two things: 1. To experience pleasure, or 2. To avoid pain.

I have to tell you, this belief leads to poor results. I saw this leader churn most of their team again and again. And now, being removed almost a decade, I can see their career from a distance and see more of the same. The reason? This leader was what I would call a "Static Leader."

st·at·ic

static leader

noun

A leader lacking movement or change.

Here are a few truths around Static Leaders.

1. When recruiting, they over-promise in order to win opportunities.

2. They struggle to retain people they recruit for any significant window of time.

3. They bring little value to top producers or producers wanting to grow their business.

4. They are typically only focused on the bottom line.

5. Their value system doesn't go much further than "me, myself and I."

6. They have weak reputations and are aloof to this fact.

7. They aren't growing personally.

8. They typically stay in small circles of people, only attracting who they worked with prior.

9. They have no idea of their long term vision.

10. Their teams rarely sustain long term growth.

11. They believe opportunities are scarce. They have a scarcity mindset.

The Dynamic Leader, meanwhile, has no problem attracting people, simply because people want a leader with a strong core value system who has *real* value to bring.

dy·na·mic

dynamic leader

noun

A leader who is constantly progressing or changing.

Here are a few truths about Dynamic Leaders:

1. When recruiting, they work hard to ensure that the opportunity they offer can help accomplish their recruit's long term dream.

2. They retain the people they recruit for long periods of time.

3. They bring *a lot* of value both transactionally (think player/coach) and transformationally.

4. They are constantly challenging themselves to grow personally. They attend events, read books, listen to podcasts, and much more.

5. They focus on people first as they understand the bottom line is met when people are improving and growing as a team.

6. They have a clear vision for where they are going.

7. Their core value system is incredibly high and they honor it *at all costs*. They recognize that their reputation produces growth.

8. They are selfless.

9. Their networks are enormous!

10. They believe there is an abundance of opportunities. They have an abundance mindset.

As you compare the list of static and Dynamic Leaders, you see polarizing opposites. Embrace that word polarizing. Because Dynamic Leaders are magnetic! They attract people through the clarity that comes from the value they bring and the values they practice.

This Dynamic Leader who understands digital is playing a completely different game. They are completely dominating today's recruiting landscape.

Just take a moment to think about how recruiting has worked over the past decade. LinkedIn has been critical for finding talent, but its role is evolving. Recruiters used to find an email and cell number. They would then call, email, and message on LinkedIn. Most recruiters are acting as though throwing non-stop "right hooks" on the platform still works. But over the past 5 years, LinkedIn has changed in a major way. It has pivoted from being a recruiting platform to a content hub and true business social media platform. Because of this, Dynamic Leaders can attract happy people by simply *living out loud*.

> DYNAMIC LEADERS CAN ATTRACT HAPPY PEOPLE BY SIMPLY *LIVING* OUT LOUD.

Effective leaders in today's digital landscape know they need to show up differently. They are following a life script over a phone script. They are, in essence, creating an attraction model over a recruiting model. Static leaders rely on tactics of the past and become hard core sales people– they're static, so they don't want to change. But people aren't buying what they're selling. You can't sell belief around who you are as a leader when that belief—and that "who"—doesn't exist.

Dynamic leaders, on the other hand, are able to lead with certainty. They are confident in themselves, their beliefs, and their values. And their presence in the digital world reflects that. Influence comes from certainty. And Dynamic Leaders, those leading the charge in the digital turn for recruiting, are the influencers that people want to follow.

MAKING YOURSELF MEMORABLE

L ead Well
Recruit Right
Legacy Matters

This is what's imprinted on 4C Recruiting swag. It's easy, there's a flow to the sound, and most of all—it's memorable.

When you are establishing your personal brand, you have to think about how you can be memorable. Think back to our earlier section where we talked about the importance of being different. Because, remember, different is better than better.

What makes you different?

Personal branding is all about establishing who YOU are and what makes you, *you*. It's what helps you stand out from the crowd– especially in the minds of potential recruits. It's the persona that you create for yourself on social media, and it should reflect your values and vision. So, when creating your personal brand, take a moment to ask yourself what makes you memorable. What do people who know you well think of when they think of what makes you, specifically, you? From there, you can create images, hashtags, and a tag line to represent your personal brand.

As you work on building your personal brand, here are some things you'll want to focus on.
1. Attractive Leadership
2. Storytelling
3. Your Personas

Now let's delve into these a little deeper.

Attractive Leadership
The most important concept, which is really the foundation for everything you're going to do, and which I've detailed in earlier sections of this book, Attractive Leadership. Remember Winston Churchill? He branded himself as a Attractive Leader by sharing his vision, values and why, and created a platform around those principles. I cannot stress enough the importance of establishing your personal brand as an Attractive Leader.

Storytelling

Second on the list is **storytelling**. The best recruiters in any market are the best storytellers. Storytelling gets our audience engaged. When we tell a story, it actually activates things inside the brain's hippocampus that formulate things like dopamine, oxytocin, serotonin– all things that spark good feelings inside our body. It's why we love a good movie or book– look back to Jerry Maguire.

And when it comes to social media, we want to fully tell our story– not just the highlight reel. We want to share our struggles, our ups and downs, our periods of growth, and our periods of failure. People don't go see a movie to just see the happy parts.

We've already talked about the "Value Gap." René Rodriguez, author of the book *Amplify Your Influence*, points to another gap being created in the digital world– one which he says was one of the biggest, and most overlooked, causes of the Great Resignation.

He calls this the "Narrative Gap" and off course, René explains it better than I ever could:

"In today's virtual, hybrid world, gaps in information and genuine connection are the norm. We don't see our coworkers and managers with the same frequency or interact directly with our leaders as often. We don't see people outside of work like we used to. This means that we don't understand others' facial expressions, micro-expressions, quirks, nuances, and tones in communication. It means we don't truly know each other . . .

Why is this a problem?

We aren't naturally wired for the current levels of uncertainty, upheaval and disconnection in our human interactions. Our brains are working overtime to fill in the gaps with narratives based on frames of reference that are not predictable causing mass miscommunication and misunderstanding."

René illustrates this with a story of a time he was at a speaking engagement. At some point on stage, he gave a small gasp and walked off stage.

What happens? People don't know what is going on, and they seek to fill in that Narrative Gap with, well, anything. They think maybe he's having a medical emergency. Maybe he saw a hated enemy in the audience. Maybe he got a call from a relative. Maybe any number of things happened.

René then walked back onto the stage and pointed that gap out to everyone. He filled in the information they were lacking, which was that the whole thing had been an illustrative exercise on how much we want to fill in the blanks of others' lives.

With the very nature of social media, we have even more gaps to fill. Imagine, for instance, that you follow a leader who lives in New York City and, one day, drops off the social media map for a few months. Suddenly, they're back to posting, and now they're living in the middle of Wisconsin on a horse farm and they've gotten eight new tattoos. And they don't ever stop to explain exactly how that happened. You'd find yourself wondering exactly what went down, and you'd want to fill in the gaps, right? You might even start inventing scenarios that could have led to this massive change.

The phrase "curiosity killed the cat" is a bit of a cliche. It's only natural for us to be curious about other people. When we have a lack of information on others, we want to fill that "Narrative Gap." That can very easily lead to misunderstanding and confusion.

This is why the stories we tell, and how we tell them, are so important on social media. It lets us fill in the gaps before anyone else can. Our audiences want to see challenge, conflict, and resolution. They want to feel like they're getting the full narrative without any gaps. When you tell a story in the correct context, that story, at a brain level, connects the audience's previous experiences, words, and thoughts and it makes them relevant to the current story that you are telling. It gives the listener an experience that bonds them to you. The experience creates trust and empathy—things that are important for Recruiting Leaders to move people to the next steps.

Again, René Rodriguez explains this principle:

"Using the methods that marketers use like video, blogs, social media, articles, old school phone calls, texts, and emails, today's leader can share more of who they are ... Communicating to their audience what they believe about leadership, teamwork, vision, values, dealing with uncertainty, etc., they can craft a coherent story about what they want to achieve in partnership with everyone in the organization. It is critical that the leader also shares their personal origin story in their branding. An ounce of vulnerability from a leader goes far in today's world.

If you have ever met someone that you have 'followed' and you already feel like you know them; this is the goal. The quantity and frequency of our personal communications to the market about how we think and what we believe allowed not only other people to get to know us, but for us to get to know each other—essentially filling in the narrative gap so when we met, the feeling of relationship was already established."

The Princeton Neuroscience Institute actually conducted a study that analyzed what happens inside our brains when we're told stories.

They put two people through an MRI; during the scan, one person told story, and the other listened. Afterward, they followed up with questions about the story to test the listener's comprehension.

They found that the same areas of the brain lit up for both the speaker and the listener at the same time. And not only that, but they also found that there was more brain activity when the listener understood the story.

This shows that you can create a real connection with someone simply by telling them a story. You can create empathy and alignment by painting that picture for someone.

And everyone has a story. So it's just a matter of identifying the moments that helped form who you are—namely, your why and your values—and then sharing those moments through this simple but impactful framework for great storytelling.

How do I tell a Great Story?

This is a perfectly valid question! A lot of people want to share stories, but feel like they're not equipped. We're not all writers, and many of us have trouble identifying what gaps need to be filled. The first step, often, is to find stories where you're vulnerable.

One formula for great, short, storytelling is a three-step process:

1. Set the stage regarding how things were. Great stories have a beginning.

2. Tell about a problem or a struggle that you experienced. Great stories have conflict and struggle.

3. Tell about how you overcame it. Great stories involve overcoming an obstacle.

When thinking of what stories to share, consider:

What major events stick out when you think of your life in terms of a timeline?

What struggles did you encounter?

What happened?

How did you overcome them?

What did you learn about yourself and your values?

When we think of these major events that stick out in our memories, they tend to be connected to the revealing or learning of our values in some way. And as an Attractive Leader seeking to embody your value on social platforms, identifying the formation of these values through storytelling is a great way to do this.

" THE FARTHER BACKWARD YOU CAN LOOK, THE FARTHER FORWARD YOU ARE LIKELY TO SEE

- WINSTON CHURCHILL "

Winston Churchill once said, "The farther backward you can look, the farther forward you are likely to see."

René Rodriguez said something similar. It's said that we often start to conceptualize our values around age 9 to 13. Obviously there's a minor range in when this happens, but this is the general age.

As René puts it in his book *Amplify Your Influence, Transform how you Communicate and Lead:* ". . . become a student of your own experience. Think about the values that are essential to you, those things that matter in your life. Perhaps honesty, family, and financial freedom stand out. Why do they stand out? Who were your coaches and role models when you were ages 9 to 13, those formative years?"

Generally speaking, the events in our lives that we remember as the most impactful are either from an event that led us to discover one of our values, or it was a change that happened because of one of our values.

So, when posting about these moments on social media, the concrete (story) is there to prove the abstract (your values aka the takeaway).

Take a moment to think through your major moments and pivots. Then, connect them back to your values and your overall why.

We'll provide some page space here in order to work through some questions and trace some early memories of your values. Like Churchill, think of this as a chance to look backward in order to look forward. We'll follow a "Who, what, when, where, why, how" model (though not in that order!). These are all known to be valuable markers used by journalists to make sure they're filling in the blanks– or the "Narrative Gaps." Keep in mind that in this case, the question of why is going to be more about why this memory matters to you. By the end, you should have a solid story—or several—around a crucial value formation.

MINI EXERCISE:
VALUE STORY BRAINSTORMING

Richard Milligan

WHERE: I GREW UP IN (THE SUBURBS, THE CITY, BY THE OCEAN, IN THIS TOWN)...

WHEN: I WAS (HOWEVER OLD) OR IT WAS (WHATEVER YEAR/DECADE)...

Richard Milligan

WHO: ONE OF THE BEST ROLE MODELS I HAD IN MY EARLY YEARS WAS...

WHAT: THIS PERSON TAUGHT ME A VALUABLE LESSON...

Richard Milligan

HOW: THROUGH THESE ACTIONS, WORDS, OR LESSONS...

WHY: THIS MEMORY REALLY IMPACTED ME, AND I WANTED TO SHARE IT, BECAUSE...

Remember that this story may feature a positive role model, but they could also be negative—for instance, a person might value honesty precisely because they were lied to at a crucial stage. We all have a wealth of knowledge and experiences, and our negative ones often impact us just as deeply as our positive ones.

The most impactful way of speaking life to your why is to share how you came to that place—from the beginning. And the key here is to share it honestly. People want to see the struggles, hardships, and lessons that got you to where you (and your values) are today.

The most connectable part of us is our failures and hardships. Everyone encounters conflict and struggle. Sharing our own experience of struggle helps others relate their lives to ours. It's the key ingredient to connection—especially when establishing your personal brand on social media.

YOUR PERSONAS

W hat are your 5 personas?
Everyone has that unique mixture that makes up who they are. The ingredients in your "special sauce" are unique to you. And nobody else can quite follow your personal "recipe" like you can. Of course, this can't be completely replicated on social media, but we have a technique called "The 5 Personas" to help you get close. And that process is simply:

1. Identify the most important aspects of yourself that you want to showcase.

2. Make sure you stick to those aspects across your social media platforms and postings.

Ask yourself: If you had to identify the 5 most essential parts of you, what would they be?

Here's some space to write those down and keep them handy:

1.

2.

3.

4.

5.

When building your personal brand on social media (through images, hashtags, and—of course—content posts), you want to make sure that all 5 of these "personas" of yours are fully represented. Make sure to include your work as one of these personas—whether that's leadership, coaching, or whatever else you consider your primary persona at work. Since that's what you're using social media for in this case, you want to make sure that aspect of you is fully and adequately represented.

For example: if you love spending time with your family, hiking, grilling, leadership, and yodeling, you want to make sure that all five of these key pieces of you are represented on your social media platforms. The amount of posts you dedicate to each one depends on the level of importance that you assign to it. And you do this by assigning a percentage to each one—up to 100%.

Persona 1: ___ %
Persona 2: ___ %

Persona 3: __ %
Persona 4: __ %
Persona 5: __ %
TOTAL: 100%

Since your business is a main focus here, you will assign the largest percentage to that persona (say, for example, you choose 30%). From there, you want to assign the rest of the percentage values to your remaining personas (to add up to 100%). This can help you identify your largest pieces (or, "pillars")—for example, your business and your family.

From there, then you can scale the rest of the pieces accordingly. If you assign 30% to each big piece (30% to business and 30% to family), then you have a remaining 40% to spread amongst hiking, grilling, and yodeling.

In that case, it would look something like this:

Business/Leadership: 30%
Family: 30%
Hiking: 10%
Grilling: 20%
Yodeling: 10%

This breakdown can help you identify what percentage of posts should be dedicated to each interest. You want to share your variety, while still staying true to your unique persona percentages.

In the above example, out of a batch of ten posts, you could write: 3 about business and leadership, 3 about family, 1 about hiking, 1 about grilling, and 1 about yodeling. It's not an exact science, but it helps as a framework to balance your posts around.

Not to mention, it can also help you come up with unique elements of your brand. Maybe you want to include a hashtag that identifies some of these elements, like #GrillDad, or you want to keep up with the latest yodeling techniques and post about how they pertain to leadership. Now you've got yourself quite a niche!

Richard Milligan

BEING WHO YOU ARE
CONSISTENTLY

I have a couple friends who I meet with every Tuesday. No matter what, we show up and are there for each other. Whatever season of life we are in, we help one another out, we swap stories, and we know we can rely on each other. If I need a ride from the airport at 2 a.m., they're the guys I'm going to call. If I have an emergency, I know I can ask any of them for help—day or night.

Friendships and bonds like that generally don't happen overnight. This came from a dedicated process in which we consistently show up for one another over a long period of time. During that time, we've gotten to know one another's values, families, and their dreams. They consistently show up for me because I consistently show up for them, and vice-versa.

The key is consistency.

Since recruiting done well is all about motivating the best people in your market to join your team, you want to make sure that your content pulls in the type of people you want to attract, and does so on a consistent basis. That means frequent social media posts that help show you as a real-life human being, one with flaws and anecdotes and core values. Essentially, hone your personal brand by consistently engaging with social media in order to humanize you in the digital.

That can feel pretty daunting. Believe me, I get it! But it's not only doable, it's crucial to build a brand. (For a refresher on how to do this, I recommend you revisit "Content Matters").

If you ask me, I think the future holds a bigger arena for marketing and recruiting. I envision one where companies' marketing departments actually create a manufacturing line to help their leaders produce personalized, individual content. On our resources page, I have a more in-depth explanation, but to give you a quick idea of what this could look like, here's an example of the steps you could take…

Step 1: A leader captures a raw video during a team recognition event and sends it to his marketing team using something simple like WhatsApp.

Step 2: A videographer is also in the same WhatsApp channel and pulls the video to professionalize it. They might add some music, subtitles, and even an intro/outro.

Step 3: A writer who is in the same channel writes great copy for it so it can be posted alongside the actual video.

Step 4: A social media manager reviews the final product and posts on the leader's behalf.

Such marketing teams would give leaders the capacity to talk about who they are as a father, who they are as a mother, who they are as a spouse, what they did over the weekend, and what they're doing with their teams.

That's all alongside things like: What was the key takeaway from their Monday morning meeting? What are some of the challenges they're seeing in the marketplace?

A great way for Executive Leaders to bring value to their people is to build those social media marketing pods for their leadership team. That way, having a creative support team will make it easy for leaders to go from doing what they're doing in their day-to-day, to getting that information into the digital world. That's the social part of a framework that I coach around, and it's one we strongly believe in at 4C; it's what we call "Social ID."

ID, here, stands for "Identify" and "Document." And it's what leaders need to be able to do to connect this all to recruiting success.

Identify content in your life, and when you see it, document it. Leaders need to be curating content, not creating content. They shouldn't be wearing creator hats. Instead companies should be building support teams that are the creation teams. That "creation team" is one of the things we are providing for executive leaders at 4C.

so·ci·al i·d

social id

verb

To identify and document.

The creative team helps simplify the process by helping leaders identify where they should be curating content. It helps prevent all-nighters, while still delivering quality content that represents you as an individual leader. We pull the all-nighters so our clients don't have to—at least, not for this reason!

CASE STUDY:
WINSTON CHURCHILL

Personal Brand has always mattered.

In the late 1920s and 1930s, after almost two decades as a hugely influential figure in the British government, Winston Churchill was driven out of political life. He had climbed his way up the political ladder and landed himself a position in Parliament, only to lose it when the opposing party took power. Seemingly overnight (while he was in the hospital for appendicitis, no less), he went from a powerful seat at Britain's political table to persona non grata. He later referred to himself at this point as "without an office, without a seat, without a party, and without an appendix."

But that clearly isn't the end of the story. We all know his name. So, what happened?

Instead of disappearing from history, he did just the opposite. He took control of his narrative. He turned to radio and he wrote articles. Not just some articles. He wrote *hundreds* of articles. "Prolific" doesn't even begin to cover it. He published the first volume of his autobiographical history of World War 1, *The World Crisis*, in 1923. The rest of the book would be published over the next 10 years, and it wouldn't even be the only autobiography he wrote in this time! In his time as First Lord of the Admiralty during World War 1, he saw radio used as a tool for naval communications, which showed him the value of the medium as a way to connect and communicate. He himself was reported to not be a fan of radio for his own listening pleasure. In spite of this, he quickly recognized the power of the medium and embraced it as a tool to increase his reach; the BBC started regular public programs in 1922, and Churchill began broadcasting internationally in 1924. He only continued to increase his reach and recognition. In March of 1932, a few years into the Great Depression, Churchill went on a tour of America, visiting 28 cities in 41 days. (Remember that travel took much longer back then!) By this point, he had visited 28 states out of the 48 that existed at the time. During that tour, he became more famous in America than he was in his own country. He built a huge platform that allowed him to share his ideas with the world.

He created his Personal Brand: one built around frankness, cleverness, and Churchill's characteristic mastery of the English language.

He became his own media company. He hired assistants and stenographers so that he could dictate his drafts and produce more writing, even when he had to work late into the night after full and active days. He published anywhere that would take him, including *Ladies' Home Journal*.

He became a famous person with a platform. Richard Dimbleby, the first ever war correspondent at the BBC, wrote that "Churchill had a ready-made, keen, sympathetic audience" hanging on his every word. And from the platform, he began to warn about the threat of Nazism and Hitler, which many people in British leadership at the time were ignoring.

In 1939, when he was proven right for his warnings against the rise of Hitler and Nazism, Winston Churchill became the name on everyone's lips. And he had already gained the world's ear to communicate his message while building a powerful personal brand—or perception—within his audience. Dimbleby went on to say:

"He had created enormous national confidence in himself. The great majority of the people—there were, of course, his opponents—trusted him, supported him and were avid for anything he had to say, even if his major promises were of 'blood, toil, tears and sweat.' Here, they felt, was a man who would say what had to be said, however unpleasant it was, and who would always hold out some hope of better things."

In May 1940, Churchill replaced Neville Chamberlain as the Prime Minister of Britain. He had built confidence in the people, but he didn't take this for granted. His first broadcast in May of 1940 began, famously: "I speak to you for the first time as Prime Minister in a solemn hour for the life of our country, of our empire, of our allies, and, above all, of the cause of freedom."

Churchill knew that connecting with the British people would only be more vital and important as the war wore on, and he maintained a famously consistent presence and quality of communication, delivering forty-nine broadcasts in his time as prime minister, all while continuing a regular speech schedule.

And everyone was listening. A German broadcasting official working in Hamburg reported coming into the offices one night to find work at a standstill. Reportedly, when he asked what was happening, these members of the Nazi propaganda machine told him, "Be Quiet—Churchill's Broadcasting."

The rest is, of course, is history.

What can we learn from this? It's hard to suppose that any of us could match either the quantity or quality of Churchill's writings and broadcasts—he won a Nobel Prize in Literature, after all.

However, he also had a famously distinct voice, one which became consistently familiar to his audience. And, regardless of his own mastery of the language, he put in the time to build that audience even when he lacked much influence.

Often, we think something like, "Oh, when I get my own company, or this award, then I'll get my audience." It's easy to think that we have to get influence before we can build our audience, but this is a backward view.

It has to be the other way around. We need an audience that will help us build influence, rather than one that will only follow us once we're powerful.

There is no one big "thing" that will create your audience for you. Instead, it's a matter of putting out as much as you can, drawing in as many as you can, and sharing your thoughts with those people wherever and however you can.

We are fortunate to live in a time when we have so much access to our audiences. Churchill had to put in a lot more leg work to reach people overseas. Writing books and articles was one of the few ways to get yourself out there before social media became a medium. You don't need to be able to write or speak like Churchill; you need the consistency and hard work he was willing to put in, and a little patience. With time, you will create your personal brand.

con·vers·ion

conversion

noun

When recruits become hires and sign on to your team.

I'm so excited. I've been talking to Jane for a few months and she just reached out about making a switch!

CONVERSIONS MATTER

Let's look at the C that everybody wants to see!

So, you've sent some messages and gotten some content out that seems to resonate with a potential recruit, but how do you turn a connection into a hire?

Would it surprise you to learn that "conversion" and "conversation" come from the same root? In Latin, *conversare* means "to turn around" or "transform," and *conversari* means "to keep company with." So a conversation was basically when people "turned around" or "transformed" together.

It's interesting, though it makes a lot of sense! Good conversation is the key to good conversion. So when I coach clients on how to write scripts, I keep these points in mind.

GOOD CONVERSATION IS THE KEY TO GOOD CONVERSION.

I'm a bit script obsessive. Seriously—I'm so into recruiting scripts that my friends, who know I coach around this, will often send me the "worst of the worst" scripts when they appear in their inboxes.

So the question is—what makes these scripts bad?

And on the other hand, what makes a good, effective, impactful script that will make people want to meet with you?

Well—I'll give an example of a bad script I saw not too long ago.

The recruiter had sent the generic message to many people through LinkedIn messages. Basically, he was inviting them to attend an event with other professionals:

"Hi! I promise this isn't a recruiting email. I wanted to invite some professionals like you to attend this awesome event. I think Jim will have some great insight for those in the industry!"

You'll notice that this was... vague. I mean, who's Jim, for one thing? And well, this isn't an email... it's a LinkedIn message. And do you even know the person you're sending this to?

You get the idea. This message was poorly thought out in just about every way. I looked up the person who was speaking, and they had written an award winning book—–so why not mention that?

Every recruiting message needs to do three things. It needs to:
Lead with affirmation.
Establish why you should meet with me.
Remove the tension.

All of that together will lead to relationship building rather than recruiting.
Here's a quick rough draft for a recruiting message based around a similar event.

"Dear [Insert Name]. I promise this isn't a recruiting message. We haven't met, but I'm a fan, at least from a distance. [Insert something specific that they have done—research your people!]

I wanted to extend an invite to this event I'm hosting. I'm expecting some top talent from our industry to attend. I am also hand-picking a couple of people I would like to get to know, you being one of them. The event will take place in [time/place].

The speaker will be [Name]. He is an international speaker who authored a book relevant to [this topic]. It will bring clarity to having success in a tough environment. I think there would be value in this for you as we look forward to next year, as this market is changing quickly.

I believe this is a great opportunity for the right people to gain relationships and market share. "I would love to build a relationship with you, starting with this event.

Would you come as my personal guest? I would be honored to host you."

Notice how this message:
AFFIRMS the person: I complimented them specifically and made it clear that I was interested in building a relationship with them.
Explains WHY they should come: I explained the event and made it clear that this invitation was specifically for them due to my respect for their work.
REMOVES the TENSION: I make it clear that this is about building a relationship, not just recruiting!

To further help you gain clarity on conversions, I'll share the stories of two coaching clients, Elizabeth and Celia.

ELIZABETH'S STORY:

E lizabeth reached out to me in July and asked if we could have a quick session because her recruiting was going stagnant for some reason.

I said sure! We sat down (virtually of course), and she told me she'd been building up her personal brand on social media. She was getting plenty of meetings with recruits, but they always went south right after she asked them, "Why do you think you're a good fit for our company?"

I'm sorry, but after months of seeking out a recruit, what makes you ask such an aggressive question? At that point, it would be perfectly valid for a recruit to hear that question and respond with something like, "Dude, *you* called *me*."

To be honest, I was a little stunned. I asked Elizabeth, "Do you really think that this is in line with my coaching? Because if so, we have a disconnect that I didn't recognize."

Thankfully, from there, she realized her mistake, and we were able to make a change.

Now let's look at another client I coached who managed to sign a ton of top talent within the last year.

CELIA'S STORY

C elia reached out to recruits and set up meetings where the whole framework was "I'm trying to build a relationship with you– I'm not trying to recruit you."

She would even give herself "guide rails," which can be incredibly beneficial to building trust. A "guide rail," basically, is a promise you give the recruit and a rule you give yourself, the recruiter.

This would be something like saying, "If you're willing to meet with me for 15 minutes, I promise that I won't talk about my company—I simply want to get to know you for the future."

She got a lot of meetings this way. They weren't what we traditionally think of as "recruiting meetings." Think again about that aggressive "Why would you be a good fit for this company?" question from earlier. That's often how we think we have to approach a recruiting meeting, but this client saw so much success precisely because she didn't fall prey to that framework. She put that company sale on the back burner so that she and the recruit could get to know each other.

In those 15-minute meetings, Celia talked with recruits about *them*.

Some of the most important questions she asked were, "What's your big dream? Where do you want to go in the next ten years?"

She was forcing people to dream. She found out things she would never have learned if she hadn't asked those questions.

In addition to learning about their external motivators, such as money or a new house, she also learned about their big dreams. I refer to these as their "ten-year blue-sky" hopes. Maybe they wanted to be a leader of their own team someday. Or they might want to do something completely new.

The second question she asked was, "What's your biggest motivation to succeed? It should be more than money or success."

Here, she learned their "why." She got their intrinsic motivation. They were motivated by family, or perhaps a sense of duty to help the world, or by something deep within them.

People typically get very guarded with recruiters. They're constantly waiting for the sales pitch.

So why did her method work? Why did people share these big motivators with her?

Because Celia had already shown her dedication to building a relationship with that person through her tone and consistency on social media. It goes back to the law of reciprocity, as well. She had let them get to know her and who she was through her very human social media posts. It makes sense that they would then feel more comfortable letting her get to know them. After all the recruit always reviews the recruiting leader on social media before they meet them.

Recruiting is a very complex sale. It's more like a $75 million software sale than a $25 toy sale. It takes time and effort. Again, this fourth C has to build from the others. You cannot reach this number of high-quality Conversions if you haven't dedicated the time to Connections, Content, and Communicating. Celia would never have even gotten those initial meetings if these recruits didn't already trust her. She had to build that trust. And she had to ensure that people felt enough connection to believe her when she told them that she wanted to build a relationship more than she wanted to make a sale.

It's possible that these methods sound a little calculating or dishonest: "They know I'm a recruiter, so why not just get down to brass tacks?"

But seeking out the truth about other people is the most honest way to recruit. I know that when I'm recruiting, I want to speak to the whole, complete, and true person, not just my idea of who they are or what they should want.

Because of this, the impetus is on me to learn their truth so that I can properly speak to it. They know from the get-go that I'm a Recruiter (it's on my profile, after all), but they also know that I want to connect with them in a way that goes beyond the company boxes we're put in. I'm not there to tell them what they *should* want but to find out what they actually desire.

And in a basic sense, I really do want to build a relationship with the people I meet. The very process of building relationships and communicating with people will make me a better leader. So even if they don't sign on or don't seem like they will for quite some time, I've still learned something, grown as a leader, and built a relationship—or even friendship—with someone I admire and respect.

This is much *more* honest than the typical methods, which rely on being aggressive and pushy. Remember, again, the "Why would you be a good fit for this company?" question from earlier? How dishonest to try to put the impetus on a recruit to prove themselves to you—when you haven't even proven your own commitment to them first!

Once you know someone's motivators and dreams, you will have a more genuine and caring recruiting connection with them. You can also recognize when they align with your company, your values, and what you can offer them as a leader. As long as those motivators continue to drive your actions, you can pursue them forever.

For instance, when I've been talking to someone for a while and feel a real connection with them and their motivators, I'll reach out in accordance with what motivates them. If travel and adventure are very important motivators to someone, I might find a postcard from one of their dream destinations (not hard to find online) and send it to them with a note to the effect of:

Hey (insert their name)!
I've been thinking of you and your love of travel. I want you to know that if I ever get the chance to work with you in this crazy business that we both love, I'll always be working to make sure you have the time to wander, seek adventure, and see more of this beautiful world.
Happy travels,
Richard

At that point, they know I've heard them, connected with them, and that I actually cared about what they said. They also know that I'd be committed to serving their passions if we ever worked together,

Now, how much more compelling is that idea than a random message from someone that's just saying, "Our company will help you make more money"?

This goes back to some key ideas from earlier:

1. People connect to leaders, not companies. Demonstrate to them that you're a leader who cares about connecting with them.

2. Show people on the Outside what it's like on the Inside. And make the Inside a place that will help them work toward their dreams.

> ❝ **SHOW PEOPLE ON THE OUTSIDE WHAT IT'S LIKE ON THE INSIDE. AND MAKE THE INSIDE A PLACE THAT WILL HELP THEM WORK TOWARD THEIR DREAMS.** ❞

To sum it all up—you've got to converse to convert.

I find it humorous when clients reach out and say, "You know, I've been working on a few recruits for a while, and they all reached out basically within the same week to say that they wanted to sign with the company!"

To me, that sounds like a farmer saying, "It's funny, but all my tomato plants started bearing fruit at the same time."

It's not a coincidence. Those Conversions are the result of dedicated time, effort, and nourishment. They're the result of building your Connections, curating great Content to humanize yourself as a leader, and Communicating consistently with your audience. When you put in the effort and are willing to be patient, then it only makes sense when your work starts to bear fruit.

Take this page space to write up your own brief recruiting message. You don't need to have a specific event in mind—try inviting someone to have a quick conversation with you. Just be sure to AFFIRM them, explain WHY they should meet with you, and REMOVE the TENSION.

YOUR MESSAGE:

Richard Milligan

CREATING SUSTAINABLE SYSTEMS

T here is one key ingredient that makes or breaks all efforts. And that's sustainability.

One of my favorite books of the past few years has been James Clear's *Atomic Habits*. In it, he writes:

"We don't rise to the level of our habits, we fall to the level of our systems."

And I agree with this wholeheartedly. Sustainable systems are the key to success in just about all aspects of life—especially recruiting.

Now, I talk about a lot of concepts in this book. Sometimes these concepts can just be about recruiting, and sometimes these concepts can just be about the digital landscape. Sometimes these concepts can be applied to both—and this is absolutely the case for building a sustainable system.

There needs to be sustainability in all of your efforts. That's how keeping up with your prospects, your content, and social media becomes a process that's—well—sustainable. And you can reach sustainability through creating systems that basically do the work for you. If you build your systems right, they will keep working while you're off the clock, in bed, or in Tahiti.

The key to this is creating "hacks." These are shortcuts that can help us get things done faster and more efficiently.

Need a content idea? Talk about what happened today.

Need a consistent look? Buy 100 identical shirts ala Steve Jobs.

Need to keep in touch with recruits? Use a CRM or tool that will help schedule things.

(And here's a tip: If you're trying to find the CRM tool that works for you, ask the people in your life! Everyone has their favorite. You're sure to find advocates for any number of tools, and they'll help you get a better idea of what will work for you.)

When you build systems, you stop having to pause and think about what to do. As with Steve Jobs' wardrobe system—you save time if you don't have to worry about what to wear, because you wear the same thing every day. Systems save you the trouble of coming up with the next step.

When you break them down to their basic components, most systems can be simply reduced to, "What's next?" As in: "What's the next step? Then what's next? What's next from there? What's next after that?" It's simple, but essential. You have to have a "What's next" system. Anticipating and always knowing what to do next is what a successful (and sustainable) recruiting system is all about.

Think of it this way—your bedtime routine is probably pretty ingrained by now. You don't even have to think about what to do next, because you always wash your face after you brush your teeth.

Your routine is a system. And that system ensures that once you've completed one step, you know exactly what will follow.

Most people are technical recruiters. They only have a handful of tools and a toolbox that they go and recruit with. I am a systems-based recruiter. There's a specific system and a specific process that I follow depending on what type of lead I meet.

When I get you as a lead, for example, I'm going to identify you as cold, warm, or hot. And if you're cold, I'm not going to recruit you the same way that I would recruit you if you were warm or hot. It will be a different methodology based on your needs and level of interest. It's something like a flowchart in my head.

Systems are essential for me to act as an emotionally intelligent recruiter. I'm not just going to reach out to you again, and again, and again. I'm going to go to one side and have a conversation with you. If you tell me that you're happy where you are, then I will identify you as a cold recruit. And I will follow protocol around my "What's next" system regarding cold recruits.

What your team looks like three years from now will depend on what your system looks like today. And if you're a Recruiting Leader, you have to be in this for the long term. You're not looking to make a quick buck next month. You've got to build relationships and you've got to create credibility. So your system—and the structure of that system—is going to be important forever. "What's next" might not come for a couple of years!

I always say: Extreme structure equals extreme success.

> **EXTREME STRUCTURE EQUALS EXTREME SUCCESS.**

When you're looking at your system, ask yourself, "Do I have extreme structure?" And if you don't, then you don't really have a full-blown system. You probably have some tactics. Move away from being a tactical recruiter and become a systems recruiter. It will make all the difference.

Here's some page space to plot out some processes for recruits. You may need time to iron these out, but I want you to start planning and brainstorming *now*.

When you're looking at your system, ask yourself, "Do I have extreme structure?" And if you don't, then you don't really have a full-blown system. You probably have some tactics. Move away from being a tactical recruiter and become a systems recruiter. It will make all the difference.

Here's some page space to plot out some processes for recruits. You may need time to iron these out, but I want you to start planning and brainstorming *now.*

PROCESS BRAINSTORMING:
IF A RECRUIT IS HOT, WHAT'S NEXT?

IF A RECRUIT IS WARM, WHAT'S NEXT?

Richard Milligan

IF A RECRUIT IS COLD, WHAT'S NEXT?

A large part of keeping your system sustainable is **Time Blocking**

Your time matters. Time blocking is something that Recruiting Leaders struggle with. It's just part of the game. And the reason why it's part of the game is because you have all these other hats that you wear. We all have all kinds of other responsibilities on our plates at any given time.

They say that the average American is making over 5,000 decisions in a day. Things have ramped up significantly with the advent of the digital world, and it's not showing signs of stopping. So, we need to adapt by learning how to best allocate our time to serve our priorities.

The key is making time for what we need to get done, and committing to that time.

It doesn't have to be a huge block of time– but it does need to be consistent. Say you are willing to commit one hour a day to recruiting. Great. The next step is finding that hour in your daily schedule.

For example, I will focus on this for one hour today, from 11 a.m. to 12 p.m. Nothing else.

When you've found the right time for you, set it up on your calendar as "a meeting with myself." For that hour, you are not available. It doesn't matter when, but you need to make that choice, and stick to it. A big key to this is keeping your focus on what you treasure about recruiting. Remember that "Why I Recruit" document you made? Refer back to it.

Like I said. It isn't rocket science; we just have to stay committed. Daily action aligned with long term goals creates success—we know this, we just need to act on it— consistently.

DAILY ACTION ALIGNED WITH LONG TERM GOALS CREATES SUCCESS

Richard Milligan

CASE STUDY:
BRIAN COVEY

Meet Brian Covey. It's likely you've already heard of him, but for those who haven't—he's a top-rated podcast host, a VP at one of the top 5 mortgage lenders in the country, an amazing dad, an influencer, and a D1 level professional soccer player.

Brian's exact path to social media success might not be replicable for everyone. We can't all be former pro-level athletes, after all. At the same time, if that were all it took, then every single pro soccer player would be an influencer now, and that's just not true.

According to Brian, the type of content where he sees the most interaction *is* usually soccer related, but nowadays that typically means he's talking about his daughter's games, as a proud self-proclaimed "soccer dad." Typically, he sees the most engagement on content around his family or traveling. As he puts it, "People can relate to that, especially, you know, moms and dads in the business world and leaders. They typically know all the different hats we wear." Beyond that, he sees a lot of engagement with stories about lessons he's learned and the trials of leadership. "I think the more natural you can be there, the better."

Brian also tries to "do" as much as he "says," by going to conventions to see leaders he admires. That in-person experience is valuable to him, and he can then post about the insights he gained. In this way, he's adding value to his followers' lives.

A former pro athlete managed to make himself seem relatable on social media. If he can do that, we all can. "I think your personality has to show through. I try to do that in anything and everything I do."

And the value he gained from building that very human personal brand online is a value we can all experience. As Brian puts it, "What we learned through building a personal brand online is you could actually get to know people both inside the office and outside the office... see what their tendencies are, what made them tick, and really build a relationship virtually."

He says that once he started following this method, he was able to hire 4 leaders in a pretty short amount of time, without ever meeting them beyond online messaging and Zoom calls, as well as 86 sales hires within one year– and he notes that that's not even counting those on the ops side.

All it took was the ability to curate content around his everyday life in order to build up those connections. "Vision, clarity, and focusing on becoming the Attractive Leader was huge, and I've shared my journey—the wins and the losses—along the way." Brian dedicated himself to becoming someone who attracted talent, and it led to recruiting success.

I want to end on a powerful insight that Brian shared. "Social gave me a chance to tell my story on my terms."

We all want to be the narrators of our own stories. We all want to be the one who choose how others think of us. Social media provides a powerful chance to build a perception of ourselves that is truly in line with our values and mindset.

As Brian puts it, whether he's online in person, at work or on the field, "I'm the same Brian; I'm the same dude."

So, to the reader: If you were telling your story, *on your own terms*, what story would you tell?

FINAL CASE STUDY:
YOU
(and Richard Milligan)

N ow we're going to look at another case study—Yours.
As someone who read this book and has decided to follow its advice in
order to become a more Attractive Leader, what steps are you going to
follow, and where are they going to lead you?

Step 1: Create your "Why I Recruit" Document

This is a step you've hopefully already begun in this book, but be sure to nail
it down! This document is going to help you, inspire you, and provide a
consistent reminder of your vision, values, and why. You need to know those
before you can start building up your brand around them! Once you know who
you are and how you want to present yourself online, you can start creating
content that is true to those values.

Step 2: Allocate your Time Sustainably

This is the first major step. Find some time in your schedule that you know
you can make happen every week, without exception. Be sure you set
reasonable expectations– remember that a half hour time slot that you can
achieve every week is better than a one hour time slot that you constantly have
to skip.

Now, slot this into your calendar every week. On Saturday morning from 7
a.m. to 8 a.m., for instance, I'm not available, because I'm in my regularly
scheduled meeting with myself.

Step 3: Commit to a Regular Posting Schedule

Seriously– consistency is key to everything we do. Again, keep things
achievable—if MWF is a schedule you know you can keep, then pick that. But
don't be afraid to challenge yourself as well. I decided at the start of my journey
that I was going to post on LinkedIn every single day. I even told some friends
that if any of them caught me skipping a day, I would pay them $2,500! Set your
schedule and keep yourself accountable to it. Find a scheduling tool that works
for you if that's helpful (reference the "Tools & Platforms That Will Help You
Succeed" section under Content Matters for some examples).

Pro Tip: For this step, I advise that you begin by focusing on a specific
platform. When I started out, I chose to focus my efforts on LinkedIn. I would
later branch out onto other platforms as I was able to be consistent on one.
When you're starting your brand, though, it helps to focus your efforts in one
place, build up your platform there, and leave room to spread out later.

For the purpose of building your brand, it's better to post on one platform
every day than to post on every platform once a week.

Step 4: Build Connections

Use some of your allotted time each week to send out connection requests and shoot a quick message to anyone who accepts. While you do that, try to find some way to build connections and attract attention. Maybe you post quick instructional videos, maybe you host webinars, maybe you start a podcast— either way, try to find some way to provide value that will draw people in. Even if you just start sharing your favorite recipes, that's valuable to people and will help you connect!

Step 5: Seek out Help

None of us is on an island. Seek out coaching for anything that you struggle with—I even hired a writing coach early on (I was a D+ English student at best). If you need to, look for freelancers who might be able to help you come up with content. Get people to hold you accountable to your goals. Ask social media experts (even nieces or nephews) to explain some of the trends to you. Build a team– both professionals and friends– to help you recognize your goals for social media.

These are the first five big steps that I want you to take. Once you do these, what can you expect?

Growth. You'll find your presence and influence increasing in ways you never thought possible. You'll start to recognize your own strengths and value more than before. You'll connect with more people in more genuine and thoughtful ways.

This is my vision of your future. How do I know what will happen? Because it's exactly what happened for me when I doubled down and took these steps.

I started my journey in 2017. I'm going to walk you through it now as a road map, and as a vision of the great things that are on the horizon for you. I believe that seeing my journey will help you and give you context through the real-life application of the leadership principles in this book. It's also to show that I walked the walk as much as I talked the talk!

2017

At the beginning of 2017, I started a new journey. I began building 4C Recruiting with the vision to start from zero, and eventually impact 10,000 recruiting leaders within ten years.

From the beginning, I committed to acting as my personal media company. It was just me, myself, and I! I had no marketing support to fall back on.

To this point, I had randomly posted once in a while on Facebook and once in a blue moon on LinkedIn. But a media company, well, they would post every day, right? I was already juggling 15 balls every day– the process of starting a new company seemed overwhelming. It meant building a new website, finding new clients, creating a newsletter, building out a coaching curriculum, writing copy to invite people into a webinar series, creating the webinar series, setting up payment shopping carts, building squeeze pages, learning new technology, and so much more.

And I didn't have a single client yet. Period! That was a scary time, and my only thought was to "act like a direct response marketer." That type of marketer would find the person who fits the client's avatar and sell them their services. Sound familiar? It's not really much different from your average recruiter. Find the right recruit, and sell them on your company. Not exactly revolutionary.

I was so afraid. I felt like I DIDN'T HAVE TIME TO WAIT FOR SUCCESS; I HAD BILLS TO PAY NOW!

The all caps is because things felt pretty urgent! I had passed on several large opportunities to follow my dream, and I had no clue where my first paycheck was coming from. My wife truly earned some more crowns in heaven for her willingness to follow this plan.

All that said, in my heart of hearts, I knew social media worked IF I was determined to bring value to the platforms. After much thought, I decided to go all in on LinkedIn first, as I believed my avatar was easiest to target there. I also believed that if I brought enough value, it would help me accomplish my direct response marketing goals.

Here are a few practical things I did in 2017:
- 1. I committed to posting Monday through Friday. (I created accountability by advising several of my close friends that if they caught me not posting on LinkedIn, I owed them $2,500 for every day I didn't.)
- I committed to connecting to new people who fit my avatar (recruiting leaders) every week.
- I ran a weekly webinar series called Recruiting Made Simple, where fo

90 minutes, I gave away my best content.
- I invited my new connections for that week to the webinar with no strings attached. Remember, the more value you bring, the more in demand you will become!

THE MORE VALUE YOU BRING, THE MORE IN DEMAND YOU WILL BECOME

Here were some of my challenges:
I had zero graphic design skills.
I had zero video skills.
I was, at best, a D+ English student who had few writing skills.
I had no time on a normal day for posting.
I had a wife, four children between the ages of 4 and 15, 2 dogs, two horses, and all of the normal stuff that goes with that. I was (and still am) BUSY!

Here are the things I activated on during 2017.
- I went to Fiverr.com and found a graphic designer to help me for $25 a week. If you aren't familiar with this platform, be prepared to have your mind blown. It's full of freelancers who are ready for hire by clicking a few buttons. It was a jumpstart for me.
- I found a writer on Fiverr who wrote some simple posts for me for $25 a week.
- I set time in my calendar to produce content for one hour every week. This was written word only.

2018

I headed into 2018 with some excitement. I had grown my account on LinkedIn from just over 5,000 followers to over 22,000 followers. These were quality followers who fit my avatar. Remember—you can see this much growth within a year, so long as you put in the time.

December 29th, 2017
I had 5,053 connections on LinkedIn.

September 18th 2018
I had grown my connections to 23,453.

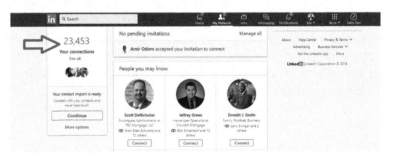

I realized I needed to build a system around content creation. I wanted it be all my ideas and thoughts—with this increased audience, I realized tha wanted them to see *me*.

This meant I couldn't hire out the actual writing, but I got support wi contextual creative, like graphics, video, and help in posting to the platforms

In the summer of 2018, I created what I coined as my "content creation box." It was a clear plastic tub where I put everything I needed to write my content. It was my inspiration that I used every Saturday morning from 7 a.m. to 8 a.m. as I wrote five content pieces for the upcoming week.

I then took those ideas and sent them to my graphic designer who would pull out key thoughts to create designs. Many people have asked what was in that box over the past few years. I've listed the contents here:

Some books I find inspirational are John Maxwell's devotional "A Leader's Heart," a book of short stories titled "Motivational Minute for Athletes," and a really old book titled "The Little Book Of Cheer."

An hourglass that I used to keep me within the hour.

My favorite snack, Wasabi and Soy Almonds.

Some sticky notes, pens, and pads of paper.

Once I pulled all this out, I had everything I needed to get into a writing headspace and plot out some content.

Here are a few practical things I did during 2018.

- I began writing articles on LinkedIn. I wrote nine articles in 2018 for my Linkedin account. These were stories around my life that I connected to my business. They showcased my experiences and were practical advice for recruiting leaders wanting to grow their teams.
- I regularly took personal pictures and used them to tell stories about how my intrinsic motivation came from my family. I used it to connect my audience with who I was outside of business. I got some of my best engagement of the entire year from these.
- I began cutting videos using my iPhone 7. I look back on these videos and have a good laugh. I used a cheap piece of gray and black material as my backdrop. Look them up on Youtube—they are hideous! Someone once asked me if I was trying to model being in a cave, and I changed the background the next week. I didn't know what I was doing, but at least I was doing something!
- I hired a professional videographer on three different occasions to create professional videos of me. I used these on LinkedIn (not the cave videos!).
- I launched my podcast, *Recruiting Conversations*, in November of 2018. I used Zoom to record it and kept the setup simple: An iPhone 7 for video and a Blue Yeti microphone for the audio in Zoom. I began bringing short clips of the podcast to LinkedIn to promote it.

Here were some of my challenges.

- I began to realize how little I knew about social media.
- My engagement was steadily increasing, and I found it challenging to comment back on all of the engagement. I did it anyway, but usually pretty late at night, after Leah and the kids went to bed.

I knew nothing about podcasting. At times, I would stop and start the podcast recordings 5 to 6 times to get it right. My audio *sucked* a lot of the time.

Here were the few things I activated on.

- In the fall of 2018, I read more than a dozen books on personal branding. I listened to and watched every Gary Vee video he produced. Over and over again. He mentored me through his content.
- I hired a podcast coach. It was one of my best moves in 2018, as it would set the podcast up to be a top 100 iTunes podcast in the marketing category the following year. Even just moving my voice closer to the mic improved my audio dramatically– sometimes it takes a coach to show us the simplest steps!
- I hired an overseas assistant to help me with my social media. They would help me by posting content and monitoring my inboxes for messages.

Here were my results.

- In the fall of 2018, I was having crazy success. My coaching was completely packed, and people were on a waiting list for my services.
- I began being asked to speak at corporate leadership events. These were primarily roundtables with 15 to 30 leaders from the company By the end of the year, I was traveling every 3 to 4 weeks throughou the US.

2019

For those following these changes, I don't want you to disconnect and think my results don't seem realistic. All of these things took time. I started out struggling with a small audience. I sat at the information highway for more than two years to get my feet under me. All great things have a beginning.

Don't lose sight of that as we get into these remaining years. You must put in the work to build credibility with your audience, but enough patience and effort will help you see results you could never imagine.

2019 is where my results compounded. By early 2019, I had more than 30,000 followers on LinkedIn. I began trimming

ALL GREAT THINGS HAVE A BEGINNING

my connections to keep spots open for people I wanted to connect with, all while my followers kept growing. Keep in mind that there is a difference between connections and followers on that platform!

I would regularly book speaking engagements through my LinkedIn inbox. Coaching clients would sign up with me because of my LinkedIn content.

Here are a few practical things I did in 2019.

- Once a month I would send something of value to my connections. These were messages like, *"I hope you are doing well! Question, do you have a content strategy for LinkedIn? I have a strategy that has been incredibly helpful in growing my business as well as recruiting to my team. Would you be interested in seeing it?"*
- I would sit at my son's basketball practices several times a week and search on my phone for the LinkedIn profiles of recruiting leaders. I would look to provide value by reviewing their LinkedIn profile and sending this message: *After looking at your profile, I believe I can help you and already have some input for you based on what I saw in my review. Want my insight on things you can do using LinkedIn to help you in your recruiting efforts?*

I have opened up my calendar after 5 p.m. a few evenings this week to help a handful of recruiting leaders. See my live calendar here: **Richard's Calendar Link Included Here.**

If you book a time with me, I will review your LinkedIn profile live with you through screen sharing. No strings attached... Let me help you get a jump start on one of the most important things you can do to improve your recruiting efforts.

When we talk, remember to ask me about these....

The amount of activity you currently have.

The number of followers you have.

Reviewing your LinkedIn Social Selling Index Score.

How your "About Me" aka summary is hurting your recruiting efforts.

Check out the included PDF with some additional information and hit up my calendar if I can help.

This value-added message created a lot of meetings and opened a lot of doors! It got to the point that it was quite addictive to press send on them, haha! And people would respond—my messaging was *way* outside the norm for LinkedIn. Most of those people had only received recruiting right hooks through the platform, so any amount of value set me apart from the noise.

- I began posting funny videos that recruiting leaders could connect with. For example– one was from a TV show where a guy set the world record for the number of glass panes he ran through. I added words to each glass door and labeled them with the steps most recruiters take to get someone into a meeting. Those saw incredible engagement with the new LinkedIn algorithm, so I doubled down on them.
- I increased my postings from once a day Monday through Friday to two to three times per day.

Here were some of my challenges for 2019:
- 1. My business was growing like crazy! It would have been easy to stop focusing on content creation, but I kept up the pace.
- 2. The LinkedIn algorithm changed, and I lost a lot of engagement overnight. I had to rethink my content strategy and move towards more video.
- 3. I found it difficult to connect my thoughts once in front of the camera. It was as though the camera was a mind eraser.

Here were the few things I activated on.
- I added Co-Schedule as a tool for my LinkedIn. It allowed me to upload all of my past content (700+ pieces), and upload them to the platform

It had a "re-queue" feature that allowed me to post automatically from the content inside the tool. It would self-select and post in the best time spots automatically. With only a small percentage of people seeing one post, it allowed me to increase the number of times I posted in a day without additional effort. I began to see my content in a new light and focused on creating "evergreen" style content.

- I hired a professional writer to interview me and write on my behalf for nine different articles.
- I reached out to several well-known publications and made it known that I would write articles on the state of recruiting in that publications industry. I had several opportunities to write articles, but they were on short notice. Twice I pulled an all-nighter to make the deadline to get them published.
- I took my podcast and began creating more than 30 content pieces from it. Short-form videos, long-form videos, memes, long-form written word, short-form written word, and document style content.
- I upgraded my webcam to a 1080i, 4K camera. I changed my settings in Zoom to capture my video in 1080i, which allowed me to use coaching sessions as content.
- I hired a filmmaker to help me create a 5-minute short movie called "The Recruiting Leader Struggle." It was a $10,000 investment to do this, and it paid off; it was a hit!

Here were my results.
- I was being asked to speak at events about every two weeks. LinkedIn was key in connecting with decision makers and giving me the social proof I needed to be seen as an expert. I had built a brand to the point where people told me I was the go-to person for recruiting advice.
- I began having podcast hosts contact me to be interviewed as their guest.
- Industry coaches were reaching out asking to be a guest inside their coaching.
- CEOs began asking for consulting and strategy, where I had primarily been coaching to this point.
- I had a company reach out and offer me a seat on their board of directors with a percentage of ownership offered...if I promoted them through my podcast. I passed on the offer. My podcast hit as high as #28 in the iTunes marketing category.

2020

This was an odd year! A pandemic hit, which limited me in some capacit
but, in other ways, opened doors. I was no longer traveling to speaking ever
but I would regularly host roundtable virtual events. I found people we
spending more time on LinkedIn than ever before. I had a captive audience
some degree, and my personal brand had been consistent for over three yea
by this point. My main focus was improving the content manufacturing line a
focusing on curation over creation. I was coaching and consulting more tha
had prior, so I had less time available to focus on my personal brand. I start
using recordings of coaching materials to capture my voice and extract insig
to put into videos.

Here are a few practical things I did in 2020.
- I hired another writing coach.
- I hired a videographer to create content that was interesting, engagi
  funny, and aligned with my coaching.
- I regularly sent notes to people on LinkedIn along the lines of, "I thoug
  of you today and wanted to check in on you. How are you doing?" W
  the pandemic in full swing, I knew a lot of people were struggling. It w
  a message that had a more than 40% response rate. I was focusing
  building relationships rather than trying to sell my services.
- I held monthly virtual round table meetings and invited my Linkec
  audience to these. I used scripting in line with my values to encoura
  people to embrace the new forms recruiting was taking in the digi
  world.
- For the first time ever, I hired a lifestyle photographer to show up
  family events and take photos of my family and me.

Here were some of my challenges for 2020:
- I had to become more creative and get outside of my comfort zon
  was aware that I had to get beyond written word content.
- I had to scale my content beyond a few posts a day.

Here were the few things I activated on:
- I scaled my video content by capturing my coaching sessions and hav
  my team extract my key thoughts.

- I began trying additional elements to add to my content, such as kinetic style videos.
- I made document-style content postings, where you upload a PDF to LinkedIn. These had incredible engagement!
- I really humanized my brand with lifestyle-type photos of myself and my family.

Here were my results.
- My podcast continued to stay in the top 100 rankings on iTunes.
- I crossed 40,000 followers on LinkedIn.
- I was now posting 3 to 4 times per day.
- Engagement continued to grow.
- My content fell into a rhythm. My personal brand required less work with better results than before.

2021

I couldn't believe it when I crossed over 50,000 followers! I was now having people looking at my profile from all over the world and asking to connect. The problem was that I couldn't, as I had used all of my 30k connection slots. I would ask them to follow me, and I would also follow them. I found it difficult as my business grew to stay consistent in my engagement with people who would respond to my content.

I hired two people on my team to manage my Instagram for me.

I began recording almost every meeting and had my team scan for clips to use.

Here were some of my challenges for 2021:
- As my business was scaling, I found it difficult to stay consistent with my personal brand. The recording of my podcast fell off to once per month; in prior years I was doing it bi-weekly.
- I was seeing more creative elements on LinkedIn, which challenged me to improve my videos.
- LinkedIn began to embrace more and more personal/business style content. A photo of your family was accepted if there was business context around the photo.

Here were the few things I activated on this year:
- I re-hired a writing coach who worked with me and my team in 2019. I had now invested almost $50,000 in writing coaching over 4 years—and it was worth every penny.
- For the second time, I had a photoshoot. I captured personal photos that I would use with my brand.

Here were my results:
- My podcast fell from the top 100 rankings on iTunes to the top 200. No surprise—consistency was lacking!
- I crossed 50,000 followers on LinkedIn,
- I was posting 4 to 5 times per day.
- Engagement stayed consistent from the prior year.

2022

All of this success has been an odd experience. This 49-year-old still had a small-town upbringing, so when people want to take selfies with me at speaking events, I find it hard to fathom. I regularly get notes via LinkedIn saying the work I am doing is changing people's lives. When I started out in 2017, I never thought that people would write what would equate to lengthy letters in my inbox thanking me for what I do.

Confession—when I started the journey, there were moments when it all felt like a big waste of time.

I didn't know anyone personally that was building relationships or business through social media at the time. Somehow, I found the resolve to keep pushing through on social media, though. I had a document written out to give me inspiration, I had people to hold me accountable, and I had strong values that I knew could help people. I could never have known I would see this much success.

I don't share this story to brag. In fact, I am humbled by it all. I share this story because I truly believe that anyone can imitate this success if they follow the steps I took. I'm not special– I just put in the work! I hope my results will inspire you and help you understand the treasure that is available when you take the trouble to put in the work. My system isn't the only way to success, but it is the only way that I think is just about guaranteed to take you to your goals in a way that feels true to who you are.

Instead of breaking down 2022 and my results for you, I want to challenge you to do something I often coach people to do.

I know digital works. I see it every day as a coach. I see it every day in my own life. The challenge, just like most things in life, is that you start something without being able to see the finished product. If you want to get in better shape and lose weight, you know it's a journey to get there. If you want to improve your finances and become a millionaire, you know it's a journey to get there. If you want to obtain a college degree, you know it's a journey to get there.

Now, with five years of hindsight, I am more thankful for the journey to this place. My dream was to impact high-value recruiting leaders by helping them build teams through teaching and coaching. As I write this, I have had someone ask me to take them on as a coaching client. I have had several people inbox me for the link to pre-order the book I am writing (I am making the last cut off, one week prior to release—I do keep busy, haha!). These results are taking me closer to my goal of helping recruiting leaders. They make me feel success in a way that is aligned with my values, and they help me feel connected to the people I serve.

This is all achievable for you. Not the numbers, necessarily (those are too, but you might not want exactly what I have!). The feeling of success that is aligned with your visions, values, and why– *that is all achievable for you.* So, here is one of my most valuable coaching exercises.

I WANT YOU TO WRITE A LETTER—A LETTER TO YOURSELF.

I often have coaching clients do this: write a letter to yourself explaining where you want to be in five or ten years. What are you hoping to achieve through social media? Dream big—if I could see success beyond my wildest imagination, you can too.

Understanding this treasure, and visualizing it in your mind, will help you reach the Resolve stage. That treasure will carry you through all the trouble that may come in the years ahead.

Once you've written this letter, go to the website futureme.org and choose when it will be sent to you in 5 to 10 years. Doing this will give you a checkpoint down the line. Then, you can look at this letter and hold yourself accountable for achieving your goals and dreams. Ask yourself: "Have I achieved what I set out to do?" Know that the goal here is to increase your impact as a leader and recruiter—and social media is always the best way to increase that impact.

We're providing this space for you to write this letter. As you write, I want you to answer these questions.

Richard Milligan

1. WHAT DO I WANT TO HAVE ACHIEVED IN MY CAREER?

2. WHAT DO I WANT TO HAVE ACHIEVED IN MY PERSONAL LIFE?

Richard Milligan

3. WHAT IS THE SIZE OF THE IMPACT I WANT TO HAVE?

A LETTER TO YOURSELF

Dear _____,

Richard Milligan

Richard Milligan

Richard Milligan

Richard Milligan

Richard Milligan

CLOSING LETTERS

N ow that you've written a letter to yourself, I wanted to provide some letters of my own. These are designed to provide specific advice to people in the different roles that Recruiting Leaders often serve. You can look through them until you find the letter written for your role, or you can read them all—there's a lot of value in knowing what others need as well.

LETTER TO CEOS:

Start with your personal brand. The data supports you are likely not executing around this correctly **and** lack the digital talent on your marketing team needed to maximize building your brand.

Your company's growth over the next decade will depend on you leading the way in this. If you model it well, you'll be able to ask your leaders to follow. Remember what John Legere, CEO of T-Mobile, said: "The change at T-Mobile needed to start with me." So likewise, the change at your company has to start with you.

Secondly, If you want to grow, you must find Dynamic Leaders. You must understand your company is NOT your product. Not that your company value proposition doesn't matter– it does. But even the most innovative and remarkable offering will not circumvent Static Leaders. Your people are your product. To grow, you will need the most Dynamic Leaders in the market. Start here. If you find the best leaders, you will have the product available, and you will not have any problems recruiting top talent.

Lastly, our millennials want to grow. They want to lead. They want more. With 75% of the marketplace in 2025 being millennials, you need to build a company they want to be a part of. Develop them and give them opportunities to grow, and they will stay. Give them ownership of what you are building, and they will lean in. Represent all of this on social media and you won't have to recruit the best, you will attract the best.

DYNAMIC LEADERS AREN'T BORN—THEY ARE DEVELOPED

You need Dynamic Leaders. And Dynamic Leaders aren't born—they are developed.

LETTER TO RECRUITING LEADERS:

If you want to grow you must become dynamic. You are the product! Improve yourself as a product, and you will become more attractive. It's easy to feel like we are juggling too much to invest time in recruiting. You easily have 12 to 15 balls in the air right now. Here is a simple game plan that will help you stay on track.

1. Identify the few things that matter most. You read this book, so I assume recruiting must be one of those things. Don't let it fall to the wayside while you juggle other responsibilities.

2. Once you know what matters most, say "no" to everything else immediately at first. You can always come back and say yes later. To become great, you must say no to the good so that you can achieve the extraordinary.

3. Focus on fewer things and do them better. Once you know what is most important, do more of those things instead of just adding more and more to your plate. Think of it like being at a buffet: you want to fill your plate with your favorite foods instead of just adding a little of everything.

4. Want to take a 12-week course that will help you jumpstart your efforts? It is available through our resources found at the end of the book.

LETTER TO RECRUITERS:

To succeed, you must align your talents with CEOs who understand they must find Dynamic Leaders. You must also align yourself with Dynamic Leaders. The leader is the product you are selling, NOT the company. Get to know your leaders so well that you can portray them as being the most interesting people in the world.

Develop your own personal brand and humanize yourself to those you're recruiting. Develop yourself to be able to bring them value. And remember— you can become dynamic yourself.

LETTER TO STATIC LEADERS:

If you read this and found yourself putting check marks in the boxes of a Static Leader, someone who isn't growing or seeking growth, then don't be discouraged. That took a ton of self-awaRenéss, which is where change always begins.

You can change your brand. It will take a lot of commitment and hard work—like it does turning the flywheel—but I've seen leaders come back from being static in a short timeframe. So here is your game plan:

1. Take a seat at the information highway. You most likely don't understand the digital world. You must learn this and learn this quickly. Seek out books, podcasts, events, and anything else that allows you to accelerate your learning around this.

2. You must elevate your core value system. I have found that one way to do this is to fight for clarity on what it is. Most leaders don't know their top three or four core values. Without knowing what your core values are, how can you defend and honor them? You can find a core value exercise on our resources page at the end of this book. Dynamic leaders have clarity around who they are.

3. You must become more valuable. Refocus your effort on how to share value. As recruits have more digital access to leaders, you must be able to showcase your own worth.

Most leaders need to get outside of their circle of comfort.

One step would be to stop attending industry events for the next two years and only attend events that will give you an edge. If you want to rebrand, you need to freshen yourself up and grow. Here is an excellent daily affirmation for you, "The current version of me is not hireable by the ten-year better version of me."

> ## " THE CURRENT VERSION OF ME IS NOT HIREABLE BY THE TEN-YEAR BETTER VERSION OF ME "

LETTER TO DYNAMIC LEADERS:

The world needs you! As a father to four children ages 9 to 20 at the time of this writing, I'm rooting for you to lean in. I know they will look to leaders like you over the coming decades for direction. Be clear on what this generation wants from a leader. Simply said, they want more than what most are able or willing to give.

I encourage you to elevate self-care as you will be in enormous demand. You will not be able to sustain being all in if you don't care for yourself well. I have found three self-care ingredients that lead to being all in for long windows of time.

1. Our energy comes from what we eat. Eat well.

2. Our mindset comes from what/who we listen to. Choose carefully.

3. Our relationships increase or decrease our capacity. They are not neutral! Be intentional in who you surround yourself with.

Then be "all in" on digital. Take the time to understand social platforms. As new ones appear, be willing to learn them; they may become the next LinkedIn, Facebook, Twitter, Instagram, or Tiktok. You will be able to recruit any size team when you let this be an accelerator for you. Use this cheat code, and anything is possible.

The major lesson we can all learn might sound a little familiar.

Be Yourself.

How often have we heard that in our lives? I remember telling it to my kids when they each started school and were worried they wouldn't make friends.

Just be yourself.

I don't say this flippantly. I know that sometimes "being ourselves" can be a much more monumental task than we think it is. This concept is especially true in our working lives when there are often so many "rules," both spoken and unspoken, about how we're expected to behave.

Being yourself and understanding who that is is no easy task.

Discovering who we really are at our core takes time and effort. I've shared some success stories, but here's a story about what happens when we don't identify who we are and what our why is. We'll call this client "John."

Last year I was in a conversation with John, a coaching client who had lost all motivation and was looking for some clarity. He was actually a referral from another coaching client who thought John needed my help.

> **66**
>
> **BEING YOURSELF AND UNDERSTANDING WHO THAT IS IS NO EASY TASK.**
>
> **99**

As I said, it was pretty clear that this guy had no motivation left. I would present ideas, and he just couldn't seem to activate them.

One day we were trying to get to the bottom of his main "problem," and I started asking about his intrinsic "Why."

There wasn't one.

He had an extrinsic motivator, which was money. Well, he'd achieved that. Just that year, he'd gotten a 7-figure sign-on bonus from his current company. But he was worried. After a few months, his numbers weren't representative of his production before he'd signed on. He simply wasn't getting the business that he historically had in the past.

What it looked like to me, as the coach, was that he was frozen in place. He was scared, but that fear had frozen him, and he didn't have any motivation to jolt him out of it.

On the day we were trying to zero in on his why, he turned to me and asked "What if your only motivation has ever been money. What if that's your only driver."

And I said, "There always comes a place and a time where that motivation runs out. Whenever you reach that number, whatever it is, on the extrinsic side, that motivation will be gone."

He leaned forward, put his head in his hands, and said, "That's me."

He'd gotten that extrinsic motivator—he'd reached seven figures, and the well had run dry.

I'll put it this way. Most of us don't feel particularly motivated to go search for fresh drinking water every day. Why? Because it's always right there in our house. Once we have it, the drive to seek it isn't going to be enough to spur u onward.

He and I had to go on a journey together and dig deep to determine his intrinsic motivation. We had to find out what his purpose was, what his cause was, and what did he believe?

I'm sharing this story because everything else in this book will return to that intrinsic motivation. If you want to see success on any platform, if you're going to connect with more people, if you want to activate your resolve, then you have to know, deep down, what will drive you: to put in the work, bring the effort, and stay up all night to make even a single connection happen.

To be yourself, you have to find yourself.

That requires a journey. It involves a process of looking inside and seeing who you are.

What is your story?

What is your driver?

How can you share these with others?

Now that we're at the end, I want everyone to take a moment to go back to their "Why I Recruit" document. I know I've harped on it, but it's the most important aspect of seeing success as a recruiter and a leader. It might be the main key to, as the title says, "Dominating Recruiting in the Digital World."

Your story is powerful, and it has a powerful ability to pull.

It will pull you forward. It will pull others closer to you.

This book represents a lot of work. It took a lot of work for the team at 4C to create, and it details a process that will require a great deal of effort from you.

If you're just doing that for extrinsic motivators like money, attention, or anything like that, then it's unlikely you'll be able to find the resolve required to make your online presence true to yourself. You'll be tailoring your posts and presence around how to "get more," instead of how to "be more." These types of posts will reduce the impact of your leadership.

But when you find the intrinsic motivator that makes you want to recruit and lead, you can always return to it. Your posts will be in service of something much deeper, and they'll resonate strongly with your audience.

Radically change how you recruit online. Find your story. Tell it. And be yourself. If you do these things well, you will experience greater success than you ever imagined.

Richard Milligan

FINAL THOUGHTS:

I know that my experience might seem a bit overwhelming. But I share it in part because the number one excuse that I hear from the Recruiting Leaders who I coach is this:

"I don't have time to recruit."

When we talk about what it takes to be an Attractive Leader on social media, it probably sounds like it will take even more time.

We always protect what's a priority. I'm asking that we prioritize recruiting because it makes us better leaders.

When we choose to be Attractive Leaders, it means that we take the time to establish our

Vision

Values

And Why.

These impact how we run our teams. They impact how motivated we feel to lead. And when we live true to them, and represent them honestly in our personal brand on social media, they help us recruit in a far more impactful way than we can otherwise.

Saying that you don't have time to recruit means that you don't want to take the time and protect that priority. But being an Attractive Leader should always be a priority, and it's the central part of how effective recruiting works.

Saying "I don't like to recruit. Recruiting's hard. I don't have the time..."

All of these excuses are agreements that you've made with yourself. Nobody is born saying "I hate recruiting."

So I am not asking any readers to make a decision to recruit more. Why? Because there are levels of agreement, and a decision is the lowest level.

If we look at this from a health framework, a decision is like saying, "I'm going to get into shape this year."

That's the lowest level—simply saying that to yourself and maybe deciding to go to the gym today.

A commitment represents more. It's when you decide to clean out your pantry and stop buying any junk food.

A commitment is more powerful. It represents taking action.

But few people ever get to the greatest level, which is Resolve.

Resolve represents grit. It represents dedication. It represents taking all the steps that it takes.

In recruiting, we see a lot of low-level decisions. We see a lot of, "I'll make this call today. I'll hire this person. I'll do this exercise with my team."

We even see commitment to those decisions.

But resolve means going beyond saying, "This is something I'm going to do."

215

It means saying, "This is something I'm going to do at all costs."

It means finding your core values behind recruiting.

It means being consistent always: you have to regularly create and post content that is true to your values on social media. That is how you establish a strong brand presence.

It means resolving to set aside a meeting with yourself. And during that time– whether it's half an hour or four hours– you don't answer the call that can wait. You don't pay attention to the 700 emails coming in. Instead, you spend that time on recruiting, establishing yourself on social media, and building your brand as a leader.

To be an Attractive Leader, you have to be an Active Leader. Instead of saying you don't have the time to recruit—you're making the time to recruit.

In that time, you're establishing yourself as an Attractive Leader. You're drawing people in by humanizing yourself. You're building connections, making calls, reaching out, and doing whatever it takes.

I'm not asking anyone here to decide to recruit. I'm not asking you to commit to recruiting either.

I'm asking everyone to Resolve to recruit.

That means doing everything possible to attract top talent and to make yourself an active and consistent presence on social media. It means taking the time, deliberately, every day, to build that presence and make it true to yourself and the leader you want to be.

I'm asking everyone to do whatever it takes. Decide that leading in a way that's true to your vision, values, and why is more than important—it's vital.

KEY RESOURCES

A s you continue on your journey with Recruiting and Attractive Leadership—we are here for you! You can find further training and resources on:

- Establishing your vision
- Identifying your core values
- Finding clarity around your why
- Social media best practices
- Airtable templates for social media content tracking, prospect tracking, employee onboarding tracking
- Further resources on creating your own growth team
- Courses on becoming an attractive leader and the recruiting process
- Courses on ways to automate your efforts
- Webinars that expand on the concepts in this book
- Special courses from our guest collaborators
- And so much more!

http://resources.dominatingrecruiting.com

GLOSSARY OF TERMS

Attractive Leader—A leader who communicates what they believe, where they are going, and why they are committed to it so clearly that they magnetize people to their cause, idea, and team.

Avatar—The model match for your team that you use to create your prospect list.

BAM Zone—The BAM Zone is part of Maslow's Hierarchy of Needs for Belonging, Affirming, and Meaning. These are created for your team through your vision, core values, and why.

Boomers—Baby Boomers are the generation born directly after WWII. They were born between the years 1946 to 1964.

Communicating with your Audience—Directly reaching out to specific people on a one-on-one level over social media.

Connections—The people who friend and follow you on social media.

Content—What you post, whether it's written, a picture, or a video.

Conversions—When a recruit becomes a hire and signs on to your team.

Digital—Technology in modern-day society.

Dynamic Leader—A leader who is constantly progressing or changing.

Evergreen—Content and or ideas that stand the test of time.

FAV Stage—the stage that every leader goes through on social media; they are fearful, ambiguous, and fluctuate between being all in or all out.

Gen-X—Following Baby Boomers, Gen-X is the next generation. They were born between the years of 1965 to 1980.

Gen-Z—Gen-Z is the generation following Millennials. They were born between 1995 and 2012.

The Law of Reciprocity—A principle of Attractive Leaders. When you do something for someone, they want to do it for you as well. At the same time, it's much harder to ask someone else to do something that you've never done for them.

Magnetize— Magnetization is where we attract people who share in our values and beliefs like magnets.

Millennials— Millennials are the generation after Generation X. They were born between 1981 and 1994.

Passion Zone—The passion zone is vital to becoming an attractive leader. You must be clear on your vision, core values, and why to operate inside your passion zone.

Recruiting Leader—A leader who manages a team and is also responsible for recruiting to that team.

Resolve— Resolve is the dedication to getting something done at all costs.

Static Leader—A leader who lacks movement or change.

Values—Values are your guiding principles that dictate your actions.

Vision—Vision is your plan of where you are going and how you are making a larger impact.

Why—Your why consists of your greatest motivations for why you do what you do.

WORKS CITED

"#Brandsgetreal: Social Media & The Evolution of Transparency." Sprout Social. Sprout Social Inc., September 7, 2021. https://sproutsocial.com/insights/data/social-media-transparency/.
"5 Trends Every CMO Should Know." LinkedIn Marketing Solutions, August 2017. https://business.linkedin.com/marketing-solutions/case-studies/5-trends-every-cmo-should-know#:~:text=82%25%20of%20consumers%20are%20more,buy%20from%20such%20a%20company.
Barnhart, Brent. "Why You Need to Speed up Your Social Media Response Time (and How)." Sprout Social. Sprout Social Inc., May 24, 2022. https://sproutsocial.com/insights/social-media-response-time/.
Brandon, John. "Author and Speaker Elena Cardone Says Honesty Always Wins on Social Media." Forbes. Forbes Magazine, June 21, 2022. https://www.forbes.com/sites/johnbbrandon/2022/06/20/author-and-speaker-elena-cardone-says-honesty-always-wins-on-social-media/?sh=30eb21037f40
Brown, Lee. "Stepmom of Cop Who Shot Rayshard Brooks Accused of Sexist, Racist Behavior." New York Post. New York Post, August 12, 2020. https://nypost.com/2020/08/12/stepmom-of-rayshard-brooks-cop-accused-of-sexist-racist-behavior/.
Bryan, Bob. "T-Mobile Made up a Drinking Game for Its Earnings Conference Call." Business Insider. Business Insider, February 17, 2016. https://www.businessinsider.com/t-mobile-ceo-verizon-att-are-dumb-and-dumber-2016-2.
Budzienski, Joe. "3 Ways to Be Constantly Recruiting Star Talent through Social Media." Hiring CA EN Merchandise. Monster Worldwide, February 15, 2022. https://hiring.monster.ca/resources/recruiting-strategies/social-media-recruiting-strategy/recruit-talent-through-social-media-ca/.
Carrier Management Team. "Majority of Workers Would Quit Their Job Because of a Bad Boss: Survey." Carrier Management. Carrier Management, June 14, 2022. https://www.carriermanagement.com/news/2022/02/09/232478.m#:~:text=In%20fact%2C%20while%2070%20percent,work%20outside%20of%20working%20hours.

Chen, Jenn. "Instagram Statistics You Need to Know for 2022." Sprout Social. Sprout Social, May 24, 2022. https://sproutsocial.com/insights/instagram-stats/.

Collins, Jim. "The Flywheel Effect." Jim Collins - Concepts - The Flywheel Effect, November 26, 2017. https://www.jimcollins.com/concepts/the-flywheel.html.

Conner, Cheryl. "How Top CEOS Leverage Social Media to Build a Following and Brand Loyalty." Forbes. Forbes Magazine, March 12, 2018. https://www.forbes.com/sites/cherylsnappconner/2018/03/11/how-top-ceos-use-social-media-well/?sh=8c9a30916a8a.

The Council of Economic Advisers. (2014, October). 15 Economic Facts About Millennials - whitehouse.gov. https://obamawhitehouse.archives.gov/. Retrieved August 5, 2022, from https://obamawhitehouse.archives.gov/sites/default/files/docs/millennials_report.pdf

Covey, Brian. "Impact of Embracing Social Media". By Richard Milligan. How to Dominate Recruiting in a Digital World (2022)

Crowe, Cameron. 1996. Jerry Maguire. United States: TriStar Pictures.

Economy, Peter. "The (Millennial) Workplace of the Future Is Almost Here -- These 3 Things Are about to Change Big Time." Inc.com. Inc., January 15, 2019. https://www.inc.com/peter-economy/the-millennial-workplace-of-future-is-almost-here-these-3-things-are-about-to-change-big-time.html.

Ekstrom, Gavin. "Impact of Embracing Social Media". By Richard Milligan. How to Dominate Recruiting in a Digital World (2022)

Executive Office of the President of the United States, 15 ECONOMIC FACTS ABOUT MILLENNIALS (2014). Retrieved from https://obamawhitehouse.archives.gov/sites/default/files/docs/millennials_report.pdf.

The Executive Office of the President, The Council of Economic Advisers, 15 Economic Facts About Millennials, October, 2014. https://obamawhitehouse.archives.gov/sites/default/files/docs/millennials_report.pdf

Frank, Blair Hanley. "How T-Mobile Boss John Legere Uses Twitter to Stay Ahead of Rivals." GeekWire, October 6, 2014. https://www.geekwire.com/2014/john-legere-says-twitter-account-key-t-mobiles-business/.

Gilbert, Martin. Churchill: A Life. Heinemann, 1991.

Gleeson, Brent. "6 Ways Brands Build Trust through Social Media." Forbes. Forbes Magazine, November 12, 2012. https://www.forbes.com/sites/brentgleeson/2012/10/31/6-ways-brands-build-trust-through-social-media/?sh=1d955364867d.

Goldman, David. "John Legere Credits His 'Sad' Life for T-Mobile's Turnaround." CNNMoney. Cable News Network, March 28, 2016. https://money.cnn.com/2016/03/28/technology/john-legere-twitter-emoji-t-mobile/.

Guest Author. "If It Takes 20 Tweets, It Takes 20 Tweets: Unorthodox Social Media Lessons from T-Mobile's CEO." TINT Blog. TINT, February 12, 2015. https://www.tintup.com/blog/if-it-takes-20-tweets-it-takes-20-tweets-unorthodox-social-media-lessons-from-t-mobiles-john-legere/.

Handley, Lucy. "John Legere: T-Mobile's Rule Breaker." CNBC. CNBC, April 11, 2019. https://www.cnbc.com/2017/11/24/t-mobile-ceo-john-legere-on-twitter-his-rivals-and-being-an-uncarrier.html.

Handley, Lucy. "This Top CEO Is Good Friends with Snoop Dogg and Spends Most of His Working Day on Twitter." CNBC. CNBC, November 3, 2017. https://www.cnbc.com/2017/11/03/t-mobile-ceo-john-legere-spends-most-of-his-working-day-on-twitter.html#:~:text=The%20first%20thing%20he%20does,seen%20as%20phony%2C%20he%20added.

Hastwell, Claire. "Top 5 Things Millennials Want in the Workplace in 2021." Great Place to Work®. Great Place to Work, July 16, 2021. https://www.greatplacetowork.com/resources/blog/top-5-things-millennials-want-in-the-workplace-in-2021-as-told-by-millennials.

Hogshead, Sally. "Different Is Better than Better." How to Fascinate, April 21, 2017. https://www.howtofascinate.com/different-is-better-than-better.

Jones, Stephen. "I Wore the Same Outfit for a Week, as Part of a Productivity Hack Promoted by Steve Jobs - but It Didn't Really Work. after Speaking to Psychologists, I'm Not Surprised." Business Insider, November 28, 2021. https://www.businessinsider.in/careers/news/wore-the-same-outfit-for-a-week-as-part-of-a-productivity-hack-promoted-by-steve-jobs-but-it-didnt-really-work-after-speaking-to-psychologists-im-not-surprised-/articleshow/87966223.cms#:~:text=Steve%20Jobs%20used%20to%20wear,It%20didn't%20initially.

Kelsay, Evan. "How Employees Influence Perception of Your Brand on Social

Media." LinkedIn, April 6, 2017.
https://www.linkedin.com/business/marketing/blog/brand/how-employees-influence-perception-of-your-brand-on-social-media.

Kleon, Austin. Steal like an Artist: 10 Things Nobody Told You about Being Creative. Workman Publishing Company, 2022.

Kolmar, Chris. "Average Number of Jobs in a Lifetime [2022]: All Statistics." Zippia Average Number of Jobs in a Lifetime 2022 All Statistics Comments, April 5, 2022. https://www.zippia.com/advice/average-number-jobs-in-lifetime/.

Ku, Daniel. "Social Recruiting: Everything You Need to Know for 2022." PostBeyond. PostBeyond, January 19, 2022. https://www.postbeyond.com/blog/social-recruiting/#:~:text=social%20media%20programs.-,2.,through%20a%20social%20media%20platform.

Landes, Eli. "Social Media Recruiting Statistics: 35 Key Stats for 2022." CareerArc social recruiting. CareerArc, April 27, 2022. https://www.careerarc.com/blog/social-media-recruiting-statistics/.

Learning, Lumen. "Introduction to Psychology." Lumen, December 10, 2019. https://courses.lumenlearning.com/waymaker-psychology/chapter/the-brain-and-spinal-cord/.

Legere, John. "2015: An Epic Un-Carrier Year in Review - t-Mobile Newsroom." T-Mobile. T-Mobile, December 28, 2015. https://www.t-mobile.com/news/press/2015-an-epic-un-carrier-year-in-review.

Legere, John. Twitter Post. November 12, 2018, 8:24 AM. https://twitter.com/johnlegere/status/1062003271491960832

Legere, John. Twitter Post. October 21, 2018, 6:19 PM. https://twitter.com/JohnLegere/status/1054165232858230784

Legere, John. Twitter Post. October 3, 2014, 8:15 AM. https://twitter.com/johnlegere/status/518041539285897216

Lessard, Kylee. "How to Grow Your Following with Linkedin Pages." LinkedIn. LinkedIn, June 11, 2021. https://www.linkedin.com/business/marketing/blog/linkedin-pages/increasing-followers-on-your-linkedin-page-tips-and-tricks.

"The Life and Career of John Legere, the Unconventional T-Mobile CEO Who Just Announced He's Stepping down next Year." Business Insider. Business Insider, November 18, 2019. https://www.businessinsider.in/slideshows/miscellaneous/the-life-and-career-of-john-legere-the-unconventional-t-mobile-ceo-who-just-announced-hes-stepping-down-next-year/slidelist/72117179.cms#slideid=72117194.

Liu, Jennifer. "1 In 3 People Have Turned down a Job Offer Because of a Company's Bad Online Reviews-but They're Not Always True." CNBC. CNBC, January 6, 2020. https://www.cnbc.com/2020/01/06/1-in-3-people-have-rejected-a-job-offer-because-of-a-bad-online-review.html.

MacDonald, Grace. "Six Reasons Why Stories Are More Effective than Statistics." LinkedIn, November 25, 2020. https://www.linkedin.com/business/marketing/blog/content-marketing/six-reasons-why-stories-are-more-effective-than-statistics.

Mitchell, Elise. "Why Personal Branding Is the Recruiting Secret You're Missing." EntrepReneúr. EntrepReneúr, April 6, 2017. https://www.entrepReneúr.com/article/292190.

Moreno, J. Edward. "Defamation Lawsuit Filed against QAnon GOP Primary Winner, Stepmother of Officer Involved in Rayshard Brooks Killing." The Hill. The Hill, August 12, 2020. https://thehill.com/regulation/court-battles/511701-defamation-lawsuit-filed-against-qanon-gop-primary-winner-stepmother/.

Moss, Laura. "5 Effective Recruiting Trends You Need to Know." EveryoneSocial. EveryoneSocial, June 29, 2022. https://everyonesocial.com/blog/recruiting-trends/.

Natalie Overturf. "Impact of Embracing Social Media". By Richard Milligan. How to Dominate Recruiting in a Digital World (2022)

Notopoulos, Katie. "T-Mobile's CEO Is Resigning, Finally Putting an End to His Promoted Tweets." BuzzFeed News. BuzzFeed News, November 19, 2019. https://www.buzzfeednews.com/article/katienotopoulos/t-mobile-ceo-john-legere-resigning-promoted-tweets.

O'Brien, Clodagh. "How Do Social Media Algorithms Work?" Digital Marketing Institute. Digital Marketing Institute, June 12, 2022. https://digitalmarketinginstitute.com/blog/how-do-social-media-algorithms-work.

Osman, Maddy. "Mind-Blowing LinkedIn Statistics and Facts (2022)." Kinsta®. Kinsta®, June 15, 2022. https://kinsta.com/blog/linkedin-statistics/.

Perez, Eddy. "Impact of Embracing Social Media". By Richard Milligan. How to Dominate Recruiting in a Digital World (2022)

Perone, Joseph R. "Global Crossing CEO Led the Once-Struggling Company to a Sharp Turnaround." nj.com. nj.com, April 25, 2010. https://www.nj.com/business/2010/04/global_crossing_ceo_led_the_on.html.

"Press Releases: T-Mobile Newsroom." T-Mobile. T-Mobile. Accessed August 7, 2022. https://www.t-mobile.com/news/press.

Reisinger, Don. "You'll Never Guess Who Has His Own Twitter Emoji." Fortune. Fortune, April 24, 2021. https://fortune.com/2016/03/28/john-legere-twitter-emoji/.

Reuters Staff. "Brief-Verizon Says It Invested $11.7 BLN in Network Development in 2015." Reuters. Thomson Reuters, February 18, 2016. https://www.reuters.com/article/idCNB8N15Q002.

Richmond, Jeff. "Impact of Embracing Social Media". By Richard Milligan. How to Dominate Recruiting in a Digital World (2022)

Robert H. Shmerling, MD. "Right Brain/Left Brain, Right?" Harvard Health. Harvard Health, March 24, 2022. https://www.health.harvard.edu/blog/right-brainleft-brain-right-2017082512222.

Rodriguez, René. *Amplify Your Influence: Transform How You Communicate and Lead.* John Wiley & Sons, Incorporated, 2022.

Rodriguez, René. "One Big (but Overlooked) Cause of the Great Resignation." ChiefExecutive.net. Chief Executive Group, June 2, 2022. https://chiefexecutive.net/one-big-but-overlooked-cause-of-the-great-resignation/.

Sanchez, Leda. "How Being 'Vulnerable' on Social Media Helps You Connect with Potential Clients." LinkedIn. LinkedIn, July 8, 2020. https://www.linkedin.com/pulse/how-being-vulnerable-social-media-help-you-connect-clients-sanchez.

Sanchez, Lexy. "Impact of Embracing Social Media". By Richard Milligan. How to Dominate Recruiting in a Digital World (2022)

Schleier, Curt. "How T-Mobile's John Legere Ripped up Your Wireless Contract." Investor's Business Daily. investor's business daily, September 16, 2021. https://www.investors.com/news/management/leaders-and-success/john-legere-of-t-mobile-ripped-up-your-wireless-contract/.

Schultz, Marisa. "Stepmom of Ex-Atlanta Cop Garrett Rolfe 'Stunned' by Firing after Rayshard Brooks Shooting." Fox News. FOX News Network, July 1, 2020. https://www.foxnews.com/us/stepmom-of-ex-atlanta-cop-garrett-rolfe-stunned-she-was-fired-from-job-after-rayshard-brooks-shooting.

Sprout Social Team. "#Brandsgetreal: What Consumers Want from Brands in a Divided Society." Sprout Social. Sprout Social, September 7, 2021. https://sproutsocial.com/insights/data/social-media-

connection/#connection-is-the-new-currency.
Team, PostBeyond. "Employee Advocacy: A Definitive Guide with Top
    Statistics." PostBeyond. PostBeyond, January 19, 2022.
    https://www.postbeyond.com/employee-advocacy-
    guide/#:~:text=Company%20branded%20messages%20reach%205
    61,would%20encourage%20them%20to%20share.
Valdivia, Edward. "Brandwatch - John Legere." Presentation.
    https://d2saw6je89goi1.cloudfront.net/uploads/digital_asset/file/10
    40044/Brandwatch_-_John_Legere_.pdf
West, Chloe. "Social Proof: How to Use Psychology in Digital Marketing."
    Sprout Social. Sprout Social, June 3, 2022.
    https://sproutsocial.com/insights/social-proof/.
"Wireless Industry Overview: The Impact of Competition and Financialization
    on Wireless Workers." PowerPoint presentation, CWA Wireless
    Workers Conference, Hyatt Regency San Antonio Riverwalk, San
    Antonio, TX. November, 2016. https://cwa-
    union.org/sites/default/files/2016_wireless_industry_overview.pptx
"Wireless Industry Overview: The Impact of Competition and Financialization
    on Wireless Workers." Presentation. CWA Wireless Workers
    Conference, Hyatt Regency San Antonio Riverwalk, San Antonio, TX.
    November 2016. https://cwa-
    union.org/sites/default/files/2016_wireless_industry_overview.pptx

ABOUT THE AUTHOR

Richard is a recruiting coach, high-growth specialist, speaker, and champion of recruiting leaders across the nation. During his time in the mortgage industry, he built more than 20 teams and held leadership positions in Area, Regional, and VP roles. For the last 5 years, he has dedicated his time to developing a system that makes recruiting simple. He partners with and coaches industry leaders across the country to help them communicate their values, build systems that attracts top talent, and position their companies for growth.

Richard speaks at both public and private events across the U.S. He lives in Edmond, Oklahoma, with his children and wife.

Made in the USA
Coppell, TX
31 August 2022